PRAISE FOR *DECODING YOUR EMOTIONAL BLUEPRINT*

"Judy's work is expansive, profound, and what the world needs right now. I thought I knew what constellations work was until I read her book. The depth and wisdom she brings is transformative personally and will be globally. She brings the wisdom of the ancients and science together seamlessly and with such clarity that it's impossible to debate the work!"

BETSY CHASSE
filmmaker of *What the Bleep Do We Know?!* and *Pregnant in America*

"Decoding Your Emotional Blueprint is no ordinary self-help book. It takes you on a deep journey to help you identify healthy and unhealthy connections to your family of origin and enables you to truly shift your mindset and unlock lasting transformation. We all have a story that comes from our family lineage and a multi-generational system that carries forward emotional hooks that can unconsciously control your life and hamper ambition. This book works with you to debunk myths you've long accepted or believed were the truth just because that's how it is in your family. As a leader, this book helped me identify limiting beliefs that were impacting my effectiveness. By acknowledging and creating a more empowering path, I have emerged a stronger leader and person. The growth is ongoing and the impact is undeniable."

CHERYL DESANTIS
chief people & diversity officer at SmileDirectClub

"Judy has a magical way of taking a look alongside her clients to the most tragic events in their lives and helping them turn the tragedies into strengths, lessons, and triumphs. Her work lies at the heart of an energy field, where all her clients and workshop participants connect with each other (and their family/organizational systems) in nonverbal and verbal ways they never thought were possible. I was so drawn to the process of change within her work that I studied it for my PhD dissertation in marriage and family therapy.

Since then and even before my study, many researchers across the world have studied family and organizational constellations to uncover the mechanisms of change and impact of this powerful modality. A must-read for lifelong learners of all ages and for everyone who feels propelled to make a significant leap in their personal and professional growth!"

SOFIA GEORGIADOU

PhD, LPC-S, LMFT, NCC

"In the book *Decoding Your Emotional Blueprint*, Judy Wilkins-Smith takes the reader on an authentic journey of transformation and assists them in unveiling the true power of who they are. Beyond your subconscious patterns and ancestral history lie a new and "bigger you." This book not only applies extensive research and real-life experiences of what that entails but also navigates you through a concise road map of how to get there! If you're drowning in a sea of how-to books but looking for something different, something special, something life changing . . . *Decoding Your Emotional Blueprint* will pull you out of the mucky self-help waters and onto the shore of a new and expansive life!"

BARRY GOLDSTEIN

multi-award-winning producer, composer, and author

"Powerful and timely! Judy Wilkins-Smith's book, *Decoding Your Emotional Blueprint*, offers a compelling new model for healing. Through a beautiful synthesis of ancestral wisdom, insight, modern science, and the power of systemic work and constellations, she shows how transformation can be a genuine part of our daily lives. Judy gives our minds a reason to accept what our hearts already know—that the power of wellness lives within each of us. This book is a must for any library of science and healing in the 21st century!"

DR. DARREN WEISSMAN

chiropractor and creator of The LifeLine Technique

DECODING

YOUR

EMOTIONAL

BLUEPRINT

DECODING YOUR EMOTIONAL BLUEPRINT

A Powerful Guide to Transformation Through Disentangling Multigenerational Patterns

Judy Wilkins-Smith

sounds true
BOULDER, COLORADO

Sounds True
Boulder, CO 80306

This book is not intended as a substitute for the medical recommendations of physicians, mental
health professionals, or other health-care providers. Rather, it is intended to offer educational
information to help the reader gain insights into the patterns within their own systems as
part of a mutual quest for optimum well-being together with their physicians, mental health
professionals, and health-care providers. We advise readers to carefully review and understand the
ideas presented and to seek the advice of a qualified professional before attempting to use them.

Published 2022

Cover design by Jennifer Miles
Book design by Meredith March

MIX
Paper | Supporting
responsible forestry
FSC® C103098

Printed in the United States of America

BK06363

Library of Congress Cataloging-in-Publication Data

Names: Wilkins-Smith, Judy, author.
Title: Decoding your emotional blueprint : a powerful guide to transformation
   through disentangling multigenerational patterns / Judy Wilkins-Smith.
Description: Boulder, Colorado : Sounds True, 2022. | Includes bibliographical references.
Identifiers: LCCN 2021044103 (print) | LCCN 2021044104 (ebook) | ISBN
   9781683648888 (paperback) | ISBN 9781683648895 (ebook)
Subjects: LCSH: Change (Psychology) | Emotions. | Self-actualization
   (Psychology) Self-help
Classification: LCC BF637.C4 W5525 2022 (print) | LCC BF637.C4 (ebook) |
   DDC 158.1—dc23
LC record available at https://lccn.loc.gov/2021044103
LC ebook record available at https://lccn.loc.gov/2021044104

10 9 8 7 6 5 4 3 2 1

This book is dedicated to my ancestors and their gifts
exactly the way that they were given to me. Thank you.
I am shaping the next chapter in my own way, with gratitude.

To my incredible parents, who taught me what love, safety, and
an open heart and mind can do. Bless you both. I love you forever.
Thank you to my wonderful brother, who taught me to think
big, and my daughter, who demonstrates the elegance of being an
adopted child and the powerful love and success that can bring.

Teresa, Kara, Keerin, Landon: thank you all for your love,
wisdom, and support. You are so appreciated and loved.
Ayedin, Orlenna, and Sennan, in you lies the future.

I dedicate this also to the ones in my family who in their
absence teach me so much about family dynamics.

Thanks to Africa for my roots and the US for my wings.

Finally, this book is dedicated to every single person who realizes
that there is a great adventure to be had and dares to go in
search of that fuller life and answer the question I ask each of my
clients: "How big are you willing to be?" This book is for you!

CONTENTS

CONTENTS

PART IV   THE TREASURE OF HUMAN POTENTIAL: BUILDING BEYOND PERCEIVED LIMITS

INTRODUCTION

One idea, even one word, can keep you stuck. Another idea, a new word, can set you free. Our minds are that powerful, language is that potent, our brains are that flexible.

People say things to me all the time like, "Terrible things have happened to me!" And I say, "Okay. And? What can we do with that?"

Or they say, "I'm held back by some invisible weight, and I'm stuck." And I say, "Let's find out where that came from and turn that into your gift!"

You are never a victim of your world. There is *always* something you can do.

Even if you feel like you've been hitting the same brick wall over and over again, I'm here to tell you that anyone can change and grow into their potential—and then soar beyond. You just have to discover and face the invisible patterns you've been loyally following that have been handed down to you by your ancestors—a system you never knew existed and that has been running your life unconsciously. A system *you* can *change*.

Everyone knows that we inherit our physical DNA, but few people realize that we also inherit what I call *emotional DNA*—multiple generations of patterns of decisions, thoughts, feelings, actions, reactions, and mindsets that quietly, unconsciously run our lives. You feel its presence in your body, sense it in your gut, and experience it in your life. And yet one new thought, feeling, belief, or action outside the unconscious patterns of your emotional DNA can change the way your entire life works. It can change your entire family system and how it has been functioning for generations.

Your emotional DNA is what you and your ancestors have brought to life through the generations. Your emotional DNA rises out of your *emotional blueprint*. Your emotional blueprint just is. It isn't good or bad. It's like a treasure map with the events and all the decisions, actions, and inactions taken around them in different areas of your life, like relationships, leadership, careers, and money, and the effects they have had on your family line—and the meanings that have resulted and been passed down through successive generations. These meanings define your reality and seem like *the* truth. Yet your emotional DNA is simply *your* truth, and you can change it anytime you choose.

When you see and understand the patterns in your family system, when the beliefs and behaviors and blocks buried in your ancestral DNA surface like great whales right in front of you, when you listen to your heart and the wisdom of your ancestors and disentangle yourself from the patterns that you and they have woven, you will be amazed and overjoyed to see the possibilities that are waiting for you.

I am not kidding when I say that the information contained in this book is transformational. Every day I show people how to explore the unique contents of their emotional DNA—the insistence that they're always second best, the belief that they're always "the invisible one" or "the unloved one" or "the unworthy one." I watch as they do the work and move through an emotional pattern that's stunted their growth for decades, and in just a matter of an hour or so, I watch them "get it," and this insight begins to rewire their brain. The embodied experience can only be described as transformational.

I watch as they realize that they are not the small, incapable beings they thought they were—that they can really make a difference with their voice and presence. That they matter and have purpose.

From that moment on, their lives are never the same again.

SYSTEMIC WORK AND CONSTELLATIONS

In these pages we will explore the power of systems, family and organizational systems in particular. I'll show you how to decode the language that contains clues to the power of *you*, and how these systems are always in service of you. You are going to discover that all the systems you are a part of—family, business, clubs, organizations, and social systems—contain clues to what you want to *stop* doing and what you need to *start* doing to create the incredible life you always suspected and hoped was possible.

By understanding systems and their clues, codes, and patterns, by understanding the events in your life—the meanings you have ascribed to them

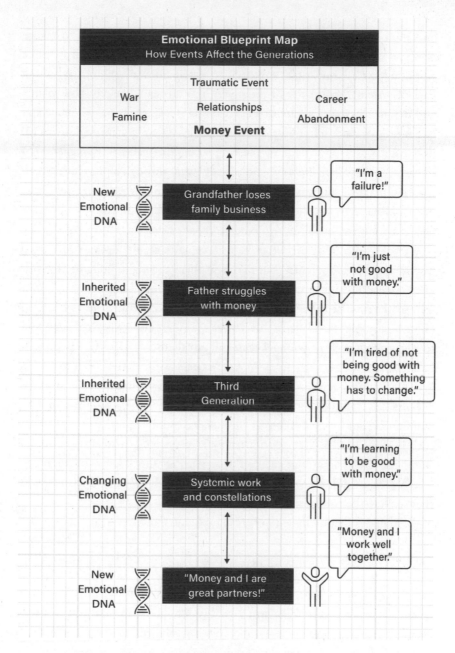

Forming and Changing Emotional DNA. Events cause reactions, which then create thoughts, feelings, and actions. Repeated often enough, these actions become the truth *until you choose to do it differently.* One new thought, one new feeling, and one new action at a time!

and their tremendous ability to shape you—you will also begin to realize how you are both the shaper and indeed the shape-shifter. Through systemic work and the constellations approach (constellations are the breakthrough part of systemic work), I will show you how to make the invisible visible and the unconscious conscious by (1) learning the language of your issue and re-languaging and reframing it through the systemic lens and then (2) dimensionalizing your issue by creating something called a *constellation*, a dynamic process that allows you to actually walk through and examine your issue from a three-dimensional perspective. It's a one-two punch that cracks open old patterns you never thought you could heal, opening your heart, head, and gut to possibilities you didn't know existed.

I once worked with an executive who came to see me because he'd been told he had a lot of potential but that he wasn't showing up fully in his work. He was creating and supporting other people's talents, but not shining himself. By the time he came to me, his career was in jeopardy. When we looked at his family system, it turned out he was the eldest child who had been told to always look after the younger ones and put them first. That family pattern had crossed over into his career. As soon as he saw the pattern that had been invisibly running the show, he realized he could look after his own career as a leader and stop looking after everyone else. It was "okay" to move forward and take care of himself. Then, as a leader, he could help others.

Transformation is a revolutionary part of systemic work and constellations. Executives and other clients I work with are shocked by the depths to which they are able to go and the heights to which they are able to soar as they explore their rich inner systemic world.

My hope is that by the end of this book, you will be soaring too.

AN INVITATION

In this book you will learn practical ways to explore your own family and other systems and powerfully transform your life. I'm going to take you through the basic steps of systemic work and constellations in the most understandable way I know. We will explore family and other systems; events, mindsets, systemic language; dimensionalizing (also known as constellations); and your traps, freedoms, unconscious loyalties, possibilities, and potentials.

Along the way you will discover how feelings and emotions are the juice that either destroys or elevates you, and you'll come to understand how to use higher emotions to shift into insight and wisdom. You will understand at a profound level that you are indeed the genie in your own bottle, and you will encounter the "sacred you" by using your heart to open your mind and access your gut's intelligence. Once your heart and head align, you will notice how your gut switches from survival to wisdom. And *that* state of coherence is where the chemistry and the magic happen for individuals, leaders, and teams.

You will finally get that *you* are a sensing being, and that you know how to use your senses no matter how shut down you may think you are. You will also understand how your body is continually sending you messages, telling you what is going on for you and your entire family or organizational system. We miss so many clues because we don't understand what our bodies are telling us!

I have had clients who unconsciously stand on one leg when they're just waiting around. When I point it out and ask, "Which of your parents is absent from your life? Whose support do you not have?" they are uniformly shocked to realize that their bodies have been shouting at them to awaken to their precarious, unsupported position their entire lives.

The body is the repository of thousands of years of experiences and has incredible intelligence. We just have to learn to tap into its intelligence and know what it is saying. I had a client who kept reporting a stabbing pain in her stomach. Tests revealed nothing. But in our session, her family history turned up a great-great-grandmother who died at the age of thirty-five after she was stabbed in the stomach. Even more common are clients who turn up with a stomachache, and the minute I ask, "What can't you stomach?" they figure out what it is, and it resolves pretty quickly. As with all information, once we become aware of it, the choice is then ours as to whether to continue to embody the same message or evolve beyond it.

In this book, we will explore the conscience of systems and understand how "acknowledging what is" is a pivot point to what's possible for you. You will learn to identify the patterns that want to stop and start for you. You will learn about the wisdom of your heart, brain, and gut and how constellations help to create profound and lasting shifts.

We have the incredible ability to evolve into *whatever* we choose. As you read this book, you may be shocked to realize the limiting patterns you have unconsciously taken on as your own. Yet you will also find yourself inspired by the wisdom of the multigenerational patterns in your family system and their gifts of emotional DNA waiting to be seen, enhanced, or changed through you and for you.

Transformation is not for the chosen few. It's been here waiting for you all along. You are a remarkable being—you just have to know how to see *you*. Once you learn who you are through the lens of systemic work and constellations, you will see that there is an incredible life just waiting for you to shape and embody it.

Welcome to the journey!

Judy Wilkins-Smith

PART I

DISCOVERING YOUR EMOTIONAL BLUEPRINT

The Treasure Map Within You

CHAPTER 1

THE SYSTEM

A Treasure Chest of Possibilities

We tend to think we exist in a vacuum, that we're solitary individuals. And yet just the opposite is true. We are deeply connected. From the time we're conceived until long after we die, we're part of a multigenerational family system that goes back to the dawn of humanity. We're part of a social system thousands of years in the making. We can see this legacy in our own lives: most of us are raised in a religious system of some sort, and all of us are the product of widely differing cultures.

All of these different systems—their unique traits, their defining decisions, and the language we have inherited from our family system (our parents, grandparents, and those who came before them; our siblings; and our children) and our organizational systems (the companies we work in, the careers we choose)—determine how we think, what we think about, what we feel, what we choose, and how we act and live. They determine the direction our lives take, often shaping our fate when we should be creating our destiny. These systems that influence us, commanding our unconscious loyalty from first breath to last, are largely invisible yet intensely powerful.

We haven't got a clue that great-great-grandfather's terrifying struggle with poverty after the Bolshevik Revolution, which destroyed the family fortune, is what drives us to pinch every penny long after our bank balance has passed the million-dollar mark. We have no idea that the anxiety that overwhelms us every time we're alone at night stems from a long-dead ancestor's abandonment as a little child. We just pop a Xanax and soldier on. We don't realize that our career ambitions started when we saw our parents struggle.

Or how about what happened to Lucia? She came to me puzzled and upset because yet another fast-growing, non-cancerous tumor had bloated her abdomen into a mock pregnancy. This was the seventh tumor she'd had in as many years, and her doctors had no idea why her body kept producing them. She'd had six surgically removed so far, and each time a tumor formed, her body would swell as if she were with child.

During our work together, it came to light that her grandmother had had seven miscarriages. Her grandmother and the rest of the family had refused to speak about any of those lost babies because it was too painful. Through a systemic lens, we know that what or who we exclude from our own experience finds a way to reappear through someone else later in the system. Exclusion of a grandmother who is institutionalized can reappear as a child who feels trapped in some way or excluded from the family. When Lucia could acknowledge each one of those seven beings, giving all the missing ones their place in the family system, the seventh mass shrank within a month. No surgery was needed, and no more tumors occurred after that.

Or how about Andrea, sixty years old, whose legs were so weak that ever since age eleven she'd had to wear leg braces? The doctors could find nothing physically or psychologically wrong with her, and she came to me as a last resort. During our session, I asked whose support she might be missing. The body is very literal in its messages. Sometimes people who like to stand on one leg or have weak legs have one or both parents missing from their lives. In essence, their legs have been "cut out from under them."

As it turns out, Andrea was nine when she heard her parents screaming at each other. She ran down the stairs and interrupted an argument in which her parents bluntly announced they were getting a divorce. "Choose one of us right now," they said to her. She chose to live with her father, but he died two years later. "At that point I had to go crawling back to my mother," she said, "and my legs just gave out. I've had to wear braces ever since." (Notice the language about having to crawl.)

"Will you imagine walking with me back to the top of those stairs and experiencing that moment again?" I asked. When she agreed, I asked her, "What do you see, standing there?"

"I see my parents screaming at each other."

"Can you walk down those stairs again, and this time tell your parents, 'I choose you both'?"

She did so. Then I asked her to say goodbye to her father and say hello to her mother from that place of empowerment. In that moment, she realized she had always had both parents and their support in her life. All she had to do was choose it. She walked out of the session and never wore leg braces again.

How is this possible?

Fundamentally, working with our family and other systems and using constellations is a highly effective method of making the unseen seen, the invisible visible, and the unconscious conscious. It allows you to look at issues, grasp them, interact with them, and move them around virtually, inspiring life-changing insights and *aha* moments that weren't possible for you before.

When I work with people to explore their family system, we surface the hidden patterns and unconscious loyalties between and around family members going back several generations. We examine the language and actions the family uses. Clients learn to create a full-on 3D experience around their issues and aspirations. Together we explore their pain and fear, the insistence that they're always second best, the belief that they're always "the invisible one" or "the unloved one" or "the unworthy one." They actually walk through the emotional pattern that's stunted their growth and, in a short period of time, they "get" the pattern and rewire their brains, changing how they think and act for good.

"Oh!" I hear people say. "I'm not this small incapable being I thought I was. I'm really bigger than that! I can really make a difference with my voice and my presence!" Or, "I never saw *that* before! No wonder I've been so _____ (afraid, resentful, anxious, fill in the blank)."

Even if you feel like you've been hitting the same brick wall in the same way over and over again—making then losing money, walking away from relationships, helping others succeed at the cost of your own success or well-being, not feeling good enough to succeed all the way—I'm here to tell you anyone can use systemic work and constellations to change and grow into their potential and their dreams. I've seen people restore broken relationships, establish lasting ones, move past their limiting money thoughts and behaviors, lean into stability, and bring wealth to their family. I see people understand origins of chronic multigenerational conditions and release them in favor of a healthier body and mind. Transformation is not for a chosen few. It's available to all of us. And when you suddenly see and understand patterns in your family system or other systems of influence, when you listen to your heart and the wisdom of your ancestors and climb out from beneath the tangled patterns that you and they have interwoven, you will be amazed and overjoyed to see the possibilities that are waiting for you.

UNDERSTANDING WHAT A SYSTEM IS

We easily navigate complex systems every day, adapting to fit each one's rules. If you are a child of divorced parents, you learn very quickly that there are different rules in Mom's system than in Dad's. You can watch TV for as long as you want at Dad's house. In Mom's house, everything is done by the book, and you cannot watch TV until you've done your homework. When you go to school, you don't take the family dog. When you drive to work, you follow the rules of the road. You don't go into a bar and pray, and you don't go to a church and start cussing. It's that simple.

We are surrounded by systems. We live in a planetary system situated in a relatively unpopulated area of our galaxy. On our planet we have created highway and telephone systems, computer systems, political systems, business systems, clubs, and social and economic systems like capitalism. Any collection of people coming together within a common framework that contains rules and regulations for its members to follow to ensure belonging and survival of the group is a system.

Our primary pattern maker is our family system consisting of our parents, siblings, and other relatives. It is our most influential system and the origin of much of our success and failure. A large part of systemic work centers around the patterns created in the family—their origins, content, and impact. Systems teach us how we can and cannot behave and how to succeed or fail within them, and they define our parameters for belonging with respect to relationships, money, emotions, leadership, spirituality, success, and purpose by impressing behavioral patterns upon us. For example, a family might have strict rules for children of dating age and follow certain rituals, such as always eating Sunday dinner together or not eating with cell phones at the table. Clubs have rules pertaining to membership, and corporations have rules bringing people together for a particular mission with shared work ethics, goals, inter-office rules, etc. In organizations we call the system's thoughts, feelings, and patterns its culture.

In a very real sense, a system is a living entity. Its instinct is to survive. Its highest ideal is to balance, thrive, and evolve, and it will do whatever it needs to accomplish this, seeking later family members when there is an imbalance and using them to restore homeostasis—frequently by including what has been lost or excluded.

Understanding issues and behavioral patterns within a system enables us to understand its current state and what's trying to evolve through us. For example, let's take the dating rules of a family that's a little old-fashioned. The girls have much less freedom than the boys. They have to be home earlier and aren't allowed to drink on a date. (These rules are ultimately about safety and survival.) Along comes the youngest daughter, and she's a rebel, fighting the restrictions, staying out late, completely ignoring the system's rules. The parents despair and call her a "bad" girl. She sees how the restrictions have negatively impacted her sisters, who struggle to form relationships, fearful of being hurt or raped like Mom was as a young woman. But the deeper truth is that the system is trying to evolve beyond the pattern of powerlessness into an ability for women in this system to feel able to handle themselves around men and form happy, fearless relationships. The "bad girl" is, in reality, a paradigm shifter and fear breaker.

Of course, this deeper, broader truth is usually invisible to everyone, especially the "bad girl." Yet those two words of judgment can end up defining her entire life, setting her on a permanent course of rebellious behavior and troublemaking or feeling like she doesn't belong. If she's lucky, however, and wants to evolve past that label—if she learns to see and understand the limiting patterns in her system as well as their gifts—she will see her "badness" is really a drive to reestablish joy and freedom around relationships and appreciate her bravery and independence.

Bottom line, systems and their rules create cultures that can be healthy and unhealthy. A healthy system encourages open communication, honesty, and a certain level of self-reflection and accountability to the group. An unhealthy system does just the opposite. According to how they evolve and/or are designed, systems can be our prisons or give us wings. When we understand systems consciously, we can use them for our highest good, gleaning the informational "gold" within them that brings about well-being and transformation.

SYSTEMIC WORK BASICS

It was German psychotherapist Bert Hellinger, the "father" of systemic work and constellations, who recognized that every individual family is a system in its own right. At age twenty, Hellinger entered the religious order of the Jesuits. In the early 1950s, the order sent him to South Africa to bring Christianity and "civilized" thinking to the Zulu tribe. However, living within the tribe, he soon realized that it was the Zulus who were teaching him.

As he learned their language and participated in their rituals and daily routines, he observed that individually and as a tribe, they didn't have many neuroses, and he couldn't understand why. Gradually he noticed that the strength of their connections to their ancestors, whom they frequently consulted to find out what might have happened in the past, was influencing what was going on in the present. He realized that their respect for the family system and their desire to understand what might be unresolved within prior generations had led them to a healthy approach for tackling issues within the family and the tribe as a whole. Essentially, they knew that an unresolved past was in the way of a dynamic future.

After living with the Zulus, he left the priesthood and South Africa, eventually becoming a certified psychoanalyst. Over the next few decades, he developed Family Constellations and Systemic Constellations. He explored all manner of systems, travelling, lecturing, and teaching all over the world. By the time he died, he'd founded the Hellinger School and written over ninety books explaining his insights, mostly into family systems and what was happening within them. This book takes you a step further, moving beyond how you are affected by your systems and into how and why their effects matter to your future.

One of the basic tenets of all systemic work is that evolution lies in observation, acknowledgment, and giving each member in a system their place. There is no judgment of people or events. Whatever is there is there. Whatever happened, happened. It might not be pleasant or kind or healthy. It may well be horrific. But every event serves a purpose and gives information. It all belongs, and when we can acknowledge what has happened as it is, without wishing for it to be different, then we can learn from it, choose something different, and evolve.

This lack of judgment is not easy to adopt, but it is necessary. Getting unstuck from patterns in the family system means approaching issues as openly as possible, exploring the system and all it contains—abuse, sexual molestation, abandonment, joy, sorrow, love, lack of love—with curiosity, so we can find the information that can help us heal. If we judge and reject people or events that occur within a system, we exclude ourselves from a possible source of wisdom—an answer to an inexplicable limitation or the directions for our dreams to follow.

For example, I had a client whose mother left her when she was eight. It broke her heart; she had dreadful fears of abandonment and was totally emotionally stuck around this issue. She didn't trust relationships yet desperately wanted one and kept looking for someone to stay. At the same time, she searched for their flaws and felt terrified they would leave too. Yet when we looked at how independent she was and how good she was at figuring things out, she could see that her mother's absence had given her the ability to take care of herself and ignited a fierce desire in her to be available to her own children no matter what. Gifts are often disguised and hidden within the pain and messiness of the family system and its dynamics. But they are always there. We have just not been taught to see them.

That said, we are all human, and many people can't immediately bring themselves to move out of judgment. Perhaps your father is really toxic, and you struggle with even *thinking* about him. However, when you learn how to see and understand what lives in his experience, something may shift for you. When you do your own deep work and your heart, head, and gut grasp what the family situation really was and see what your father was experiencing that made him so toxic, you may be able to accept the new context this deeper dimension of information creates. Doing so can prompt a new truth for you that allows you to shift . . . which is the whole point. Otherwise, you, too, may unconsciously follow the pattern and become toxic.

It's not about your mom or dad or whomever. It's about *you*. When you shift your thoughts and understanding, you can escape ancient history and begin creating new emotional DNA. In doing this, you are also giving part of your emotional blueprint a different meaning and potential outcome. After that, your relationship with your family system and its members—and with yourself—will no longer be the same.

CONSCIENCE OF THE SYSTEM

In systemic work, we call the various rules and regulations unique to each system the "conscience of the system." When we look at the effects of the personal conscience, we see that they are similar to the unwritten rules in a company. You obey them, you thrive; you buck them, you feel at risk. We've already pointed out some examples—lights out by ten, no dates on school nights, no snacking between meals, etc. The paradox is that very often for a system to grow, at least one of its members has to risk so-called "bad conscience" by breaking its rules; otherwise, always sticking to the rules, doing more of the same, keeps you and the system exactly where you are: stuck. Hence, the risk-averse company has to learn to take calculated risks, and one brave family member has to consciously make a choice to break generations of silence and marginalization.

For example, perhaps your mother insisted on you always writing thank-you notes for gifts received on birthdays and Christmas before you'd even gotten to play with your new toys. Fast forward twenty years, and you're exhausted, staying up until the wee hours handling your perceived social obligations. There is no thought of your own pleasure; rather, you focus on belonging by being the good kid in compliance with the system rules. Moving into "bad conscience" and letting notes and other responses to people slide for a day is a move in a healthier, freer direction within the pattern of the family system.

The trick is learning to acknowledge and respect what's already there while figuring out how to act differently in service of both yourself and the system of which you are a part. In the above example, maybe letter writing led to a talent in written communication, which led to a career in journalism. Deadlines are a big deal. Thanks, Mom! That is a healthy gift that a particular systemic rule bestowed. But if the old rule continues to exhaust you because you feel obligated to keep up with unnecessary and outdated social niceties, it becomes detrimental. There is no conscious evolution.

The rule dominates, and you don't look further. And when the rules dominate at the cost of growth, we end up falling into something called a systemic trance.

Family systems can offer an opportunity for the soul to evolve but can just as easily cause it to fall asleep and hibernate. When we succumb to the familiarity of the system and tell ourselves, "That's just the way things are," we are basically in a systemic trance. "Women cook and do the housework. That's just the way things are. Men work until they drop to put food on the table and keep the family safe. That's just the way things are." (Yes, here in the twenty-first century, I constantly see both men and women of all ages caught in this ancient gender-role trance.)

The status quo is familiar and comforting. In a trance, you don't have to think; you just unconsciously follow the system's rules. But the status quo also keeps you stuck or hitting brick walls you don't understand and can't seem to move beyond—until you know what to look for. Let's say in your family everybody drinks alcohol. The first forty years of your life, you live in the systemic trance of alcohol . . . until one day you decide it's time to create a healthier lifestyle for yourself, and you stop drinking. Yet you find yourself struggling not to join the family in a drink when you visit on weekends. It bothers you that you haven't fully committed to your health; at the same time, it's so much easier to fit in if you drink when they do. Bottom line, the need to belong to the family system is greater than the desire to be healthy and thrive.

The comfort of the trance and the need to belong are often at the root of people's failed ventures or a failure to change. Even when a client says they want to change something and genuinely mean it, often the desire is not enough to break the chains of the need to belong at any cost. When that happens, they have to build a stronger case for their dreams and heart's desires than the systemic rules that limit them.

If systemic patterns go unrecognized, we can form unconscious loyalties to members or rules of the system such that we stick to them at the cost of our own fortune or health. One of my favorite examples is a military man who came in to see me. He said he was in big trouble. I asked what the problem was, and he said, "They want to promote me to a colonel."

"Okay, I'm lost," I said. "How is this a problem?"

"You don't understand. My father was a major. My grandfather was a major. My great-grandfather was a major. They want to make me a *colonel*."

I asked why this was so bad, and his face paled. He said, "They were all fine men. How dare I be bigger than them?"

As we explored his family system, he explained that his great-grand-father had been very clear that "a major is plenty enough for this family!" My client had formed such a tight loyalty to those who came before him that the idea of doing better than his forebears threw him into a panic. He didn't know if he deserved to be "better," and he was terrified of the cost if he took that step.

I asked him how it might feel if he thanked his male lineage for a legacy so strong that he could take that legacy even further and hold a good place in the military as a colonel. That worked for him, and he could settle into the idea of his promotion. But notice how loyalty to that one sentence had kept all the men of the family smaller than they might have been for four generations!

Such is the power of the trance, our loyalty to the system, and our need to belong.

SYSTEMIC SENTENCES

As we have just seen, there are sayings in every family. Systemic sentences are the things we tell ourselves over and over again and believe are true, things our family system may have been telling its members for generations. Perhaps some of the following examples will sound familiar to you.

- Education is better than money.

- Familiarity breeds contempt.

- You can have love or money, but not both.

- Hard work creates an honest man.

- Too much success may cost you everything.

- You can't teach an old dog new tricks.

- Blood is thicker than water.

Every system has systemic sentences about success, failure, love, relationships, money, leadership, careers, health, age . . . everything under the sun. As a member of a family system, because of constant exposure to these sayings, you came to believe they were *the* truth when in fact they're just one way of seeing the world. They're just the family system's truth, and now yours. And you can change them any time you want.

Systemic sentences quite literally run our lives, and we will talk about them a lot throughout this book. Once these sentences are identified and their origins and effects explored, we can use them to liberate ourselves from the multigenerational patterns we have mistaken for our own current reality.

GUIDING PRINCIPLES IN SYSTEMIC WORK AND CONSTELLATIONS

The systemic work developed by Bert Hellinger has three principles[1] that are always in play and important to know if you want to use this work for yourself or learn how to facilitate it with others. Any issue you or a client is faced with will fall into one of these three principles. Once you identify which principle is in play, you will have a broad idea of the area that needs to be addressed and how it needs to be resolved. With these three principles, you can very quickly begin to understand how to navigate the systemic world at a simple level that's usable in your day-to-day life.

> **1st Principle: Belonging.** Everybody has a right to belong.
> Every single event, every member, every decision belongs because each one shapes the system that shapes you. This includes your lecherous Uncle Harry, your alcoholic sister, and your black-sheep brother. Good, bad, indifferent, up, down, and sideways, everyone counts because everyone brings information into the system that is needed for the people in the system and the system itself to evolve and thrive. Yet sometimes family members are excluded because including them is too emotionally difficult, like we saw with Lucia's grandmother who had seven miscarriages. But as we also saw, just because those miscarried beings were ignored didn't mean they didn't exist and that their influence had gone away.

Judgment and fear are often in play when we try to exclude someone from the system. I hear clients say things like, "We don't talk about grandmother much. She gambled and almost lost everything." Then they wonder why their child has an addiction or a total aversion to gambling.

We all want to belong, to be accepted and included. When we're excluded, we experience all sorts of negative thoughts and emotions. Yet when we try to fit in, we sometimes compromise ourselves. In this scenario, you want to look at what about belonging is not working for you and how to resolve that. You want to explore the origins of that sense of "not belonging" and see if it belongs to you or the whole family system.

If you struggle to belong or you belong in a way that is limiting, how can you create belonging in a way that brings you joy and strength? Maybe you belong in the family by being quiet like everyone else so that you fit in, but there's a part of you that's itching to be the happy extrovert you are by nature. And yet you are afraid that this may cause exclusion. If you can see how to belong in a way that acknowledges the quietness in the family yet allows you to shine, you expand the system and belong by being the authentic pioneer who grows the system.

2nd Principle: Place and order. This refers to your exact place in your family or organizational system, for example, the eldest child or the senior vice president. In your family system, this place is fixed. In an organization, it can change. Perhaps you had to take care of your siblings as a child, maybe even your parents. If so, you were giving to those from whom you should receive, and that puts you out of place and order. This may lead you to always be the one taking care of things and, in a sense, having to be too "big" all the time. This can, in turn, result in feeling like you never receive what you need. When you can learn to take your place and acknowledge but not take on everyone else's stuff, order is restored. Stepping back into place often creates a sense of lightness, freedom, and possibility.

Conversely, if you gave up your position to another sibling or family member who needed more, perhaps you are now too small and often feel invisible, unable to receive your full measure of life, flow, love, success. You see this sometimes in leaders who insist on being invisible. They promote others, which is great, but do not take their own place.

If anybody's right to belong is denied for any reason, this creates an out-of-orderness in the system and somebody from a later generation may begin to exhibit similar lifestyles, habits, thoughts, feelings, or patterns to the one who was excluded *as though they were their own*. Back to the example of Lucia. Systems themselves are dynamic and all-inclusive and always seek to restore belonging, harmony, and balance when it is absent. In Lucia's case, her seven tumors were clearly showing what had been excluded, ensuring that all were included and "re-membered."

There are roles and rankings in all systems. In family systems, great-grandparents come first (or great-great-great-grandparents or prior ancestors), then the grandparents and the parents. Those who came first carry more life weight simply because life came to them first. That's all. Ranking doesn't make you or anyone else better or worse. We each have our place in a system, and only our place. When we know and stand in our own place, we receive what we need and can pass on what we should. Life, love, and success can flow. When we are out of place, we feel it in the ways we don't belong, and life doesn't flow as it should. We can feel limited, burdened, or cheated. In organizations, there are many different ways to rank. It can be by skill set, by age, by tenure, by flow, by customer weight, or by salary, for example.

3rd Principle: Balance of give and receive. Are you giving too much love, money, time, attention, or ___ (fill in the blank) and not receiving in return? This dynamic kills many a relationship in any system. The flip side of this principle is taking too much. Systems and people thrive where there is balance and falter when it is absent.

In one organization I worked with, everybody was working well together until the boss took away vacation days. Almost immediately, everybody started indiscriminately taking sick days. What were the members of the system saying? *The balance of give and receive in the system is not okay. It's asking too much of us without giving enough in return. So, now we're going to take sick days.*

WHEN YOU DON'T KNOW MUCH ABOUT YOUR FAMILY OF ORIGIN

Many times people who haven't been connected to their families of origin are stunned by the parallels in their lives when they do finally connect. We don't see the individual strands of physical DNA, we aren't even conscious of them, but we express their patterns clearly, and emotional DNA is no different. You contain all that you need to move forward—you just have to know how to see it.

At one of my events, Lisa stood up and proclaimed that this wasn't for her. She was adopted and had no connection to her family of origin, and the tears in her eyes showed how painful this was for her. I invited her to work with me. To one side of the room was a mirror, and I asked her to take a look and tell me how she was different physically from her adoptive family. Then I asked how her personality was different from her adoptive family's and what her frustrations and deep desires were, and bit by bit Lisa realized that she had all that she needed, including a stronger connection to her biological parents than she had thought possible. With one new thought and feeling, she began connecting in different ways. I suggested that she write down all her frustrations, heart's desires, and significant events in her life and look for the patterns that kept her stuck. The patterns came from somewhere, and they were trying to evolve through her dreams and desires—she didn't need to know the details about her family of origin. Through her own frustrations, dreams, and desires, Lisa could feel a connection and a sense of destiny.

Systemic work and constellations doesn't preclude those who are adopted, orphaned, estranged, or who don't know much about their family of origin. You don't need a family tree hanging on the wall to tell you who you are. Your patterns of thought, feelings, actions, and inactions are the clues that provide insights into your heritage. Strong points of view, inexplicable dogmatism, phobias, and innate emotional habits are clues to what lives in your system and where those traits may have originated.

In systems, it's not just multiple generations that give us clues. Our own words, feelings, and mindsets and the meanings we have made of events in our own lives give us a clear idea of where and how we are stuck and where we are driven or pulled to go. What situations repeat for you? In what places have you consistently gotten stuck? What stories do you tell yourself about your abilities and potential? Outmoded patterns that no longer work for you and the new patterns that want to surface are there, even though you have no clear family history.

You may never find the ancestor who first sparked the patterns of fear and doubt or determination and integrity, but you will find ways to acknowledge the patterns and then embrace what does work while laying down the old patterns that do not serve, turning them into places of wisdom. There is the seed of greatness in you, and as you sow it and begin to change, not only do you rise and transform, but you lay the path for those who come after you while connecting to the invisible ones who came before.

Remember, if you are adopted, you have twice the field and energetic flow—once from your biological parents and the second time from the parents who chose you. You don't have less, you have more. You know the gifts your adoptive parents gave you. What are the gifts your biological parents passed on? Did it take courage to have you and give you up? Selflessness? What other gifts did they pass on that you have not considered? Your strength? Your smile? Your humor? Your gift of music?

Systemic patterns pass on to you whether you are conscious of them or not. You have only to watch shows like *Long Lost Family* to see how patterns repeat. Even when we don't know our family of origin growing up, it's surprising to find how much of their history we have repeated without even knowing them.

Systemic Steppingstone #1:
Discovering Your Family System

Discovering your family system is like exploring a treasure map. All the clues to the places you are stuck and the destiny that's trying to emerge through you are contained in the clues within your family system. It's helpful to keep a journal of this journey. As the pieces of your document come together, the path, possibilities, and treasure emerge. The gifts that belong to only you are revealed, waiting for you to turn what looks like a broken mess into an incredible journey. Anger in a family becomes peace through you. Generations of a marginalized group find a champion in the hardworking, scrappy kid who fights their way to the top.

A great first step toward understanding your family system and yourself is to set aside some focus time to be fully present and look at your family in light of the three principles of (1) belonging, (2) order, and (3) balance of give and receive. Are there family members who clearly demonstrate an issue with any of these principles?

For example: Does your sister act out because she feels like she doesn't belong? Did your dad have to step into his father's shoes at an early age and take care of the family? If so, do you, too, find yourself overburdened with responsibilities? Do you chronically try to take on too much in unconscious loyalty to your dad, who was forced out of order in the family system? Or are you someone who plays too small? Does your mother give a lot of emotional support and nurturing and yet receive little in return from her spouse or family? Do you find yourself emulating that pattern? Maybe you're not compensated well for all the responsibility and work you do in business? Perhaps you find yourself in relationships where the balance of emotional give and receive is off?

Look for patterns related to the three principles and their influences on you. And if you have no family or no family information, look for these patterns in your immediate events, relationships, or chosen family.

Systemic Steppingstone #2: Uncovering Your Systemic Sentences

List all the family truisms, all those systemic sentences that you heard and adopted as your own. Perhaps you find yourself saying these same things to your children. Once you have your list, notice the way you have lived your life. Think about the choices made and not made. How much has your life been shaped by these sentences in your head and what you have made them mean? How have they limited or supported you?

These are what unconsciously run the show, and we will explore them in more depth later in the book. A hint here is to look at what is said in the family about things like careers, relationships, fear, purpose, guilt, success, failure, illness, money, and other significant aspects of your family.

CHAPTER 2

YOUR HIDDEN TREASURE IN 3D

Emotional DNA and Constellations

My family is cursed." I've had several clients make that statement. It seems an extreme declaration until we realize that research shows that patterns of thoughts, feelings, actions, and even events in areas like health, relationships, and leadership can be passed down through the generations. I see it play out in families who struggle with certain issues like lack of education, dysfunctional relationships, addiction, failure in careers, or an inability to create financial success. It is not a curse, it's an inheritance.

I call this inheritance your emotional DNA, and it is based on your interpretation of the events in the emotional blueprint of your family system.

Your emotional DNA is expressed very strongly in your thoughts, words, tone, and meaning-making. The language that you speak creates your truth, direction, purpose, sense of self, and sense of others. It creates your future, whether successful, mediocre, or dismal. Your family system's emotional DNA is also felt very strongly in your body, even when you're not aware of it. The feelings that arise as part of a system give us a strong internal compass to steer by. We know we're in or out of alignment with our family or organizational systems because we can feel it. We know we're in bad conscience with the system because we feel it. We know when we belong or when we're being excluded because we feel it.

When we feel respected and acknowledged within a system, we're more inclined to open up, share, pass on wisdom, and engage with the system because we feel we have something of value to offer. Our discretionary energy and passion come out and we engage. When we feel like we don't belong or like we're not smart enough or funny enough, we feel fragile and at risk and withdraw.

An entire system may have a feeling or sensing pattern running through it, like guilt, that stems from a single event or series of events in the past. When we look back through the generations, we can often see how or where a pattern that now lives in *our* thoughts, feelings, and actions, limiting our personal and professional lives, may have been created and imprinted on the system's emotional DNA.

Dan, a successful businessman, came to me complaining about feeling driven to work to exhaustion. "My father and grandfather worked three jobs to support us and give me an opportunity in life," he said. "I'm now doing very well as an entrepreneur, but I feel like I am not working hard enough. I feel like I should take on another job. But I'm already exhausted by the end of the day."

As we worked through his current state and history, he acknowledged he was already earning exceptionally well and that an extra job wouldn't make much of a difference to his bottom line. Taking another job was simply perpetuating the ingrained habits of his system and his father's driving emotions of fear and determination to support the family. His body was saying, "No! Please. Stop and do life differently!"

I told him, "If you continue to work that hard, even with success, you teach your children that play is not an option. You teach them that hard work is an end in itself that reaps no reward." As he learned to reframe the hard work of his grandfather and father, he realized they had paved the way for him to create a family where success and money were finally fully realized and relaxation and play were welcomed as new members. I asked him what might happen if he took some of the money he had earned, invested it in a really nice vacation, and invited his father and grandfather to come along. He did so and celebrated them both at a family dinner, and by paying off his father's home and buying new furniture for his grandfather. The pattern of driven determination and intense work was no longer needed, and the pattern of play and generosity could emerge once he could see how important it was to transform the pattern.

Few people have trouble imagining that emotional patterns can be passed down in a family. But sometimes the repeating pattern in a family system is an event, complete with the accompanying emotional disturbances. Some of these events can be almost too bizarre to believe.

For example, I had a client who fearfully reported that he was sure he was going to lose a leg and become an amputee. This would seem to be a wildly unlikely possibility—an irrational phobia showing up out of nowhere. But diving into his family history, I learned that every male in his family system for seven generations had lost their right leg one way or another. It had started with a great-grandfather several times removed. By engaging multiple senses and setting up multiple generations in a constellation (the 3D process explained later in this chapter), he was able to obtain a broader view of his family's system dynamics, which led to insights and shifts that enabled him to change his thinking that losing a leg was inevitable. By rewiring his brain and body, he healed "the curse" and is still walking on two legs to this day.

AN EVOLUTIONARY MANDATE

I mentioned in the last chapter that all systems, family and otherwise, first look to survive and *then* to thrive. The emotional blueprint is just there; what is touched into life is your emotional DNA along with all its hidden origins and impacts *and* your deep desire to find and grow your own destiny. Once you decode the clues to your limitations and places where you are stuck, you are free to consciously create a new pattern with new results. It takes understanding the existing blueprint to create new emotional DNA. It wants to mature just as much as our physical DNA wants to carry out life's mandate to evolve. Systems have their own aggregate intelligence and, through their individual members, are always seeking to improve conditions, thus ensuring the survival and welfare of future generations.

I remember a young woman who came to see me because she desperately wanted to be happy. When I asked her what "happy" looked like, she said it meant that she didn't have to be frightened of losing someone all the time.

"Who have you lost?" I asked.

"Nobody," she said. "But it's just a matter of time."

Further inquiry revealed that her great-grandmother had lost a number of children, and so had her mother. This client was too scared to even date, subconsciously knowing what would inevitably follow. I asked her what might have caused the losses, and she said there was a specific condition that ran in her family that predisposes women to miscarry. She had never talked to a doctor about this, but after our session she agreed to seek out professional advice.

Later, she excitedly reported back that she had learned there was an effective treatment that had not been available to prior generations. Her fear of loss decreased, and she began to engage with more people socially. Her desire for something more had driven her to look for a solution that hadn't existed for the other women in her lineage. With the solution came the resolution of the fear and the possibility of engaging with life. The pattern of fear could rest, replaced by a pattern of hope and birth. It should be noted here that this process often takes time. The unconscious loyalty to the ancestors is so strong that it needs to be acknowledged and integrated before you can move forward. It has its place, and to simply disregard the place of what's not wanted can create a default back to the old pattern.

Systems evolve. What looks like a train wreck in this generation may have originally been a solution for something else in another generation, a pattern that has now outlived its usefulness. We can remain victims and spend our lives saying, "It's all my mother's fault." We can take the easy path of blame and choose not to see what's really living through us. Or we can respond to the driving thoughts and internal feelings of our emotional DNA, listen to the inner voices, understand what previous generations were dealing with, look at what's trying to emerge through our hearts' desires, goals, and purpose, and move forward even more swiftly.

It's not just individuals and organizations that are caught in systems. Whole cultures are subject to the same dynamic. If we look at history and explore its events, we can see the patterns of thoughts, feelings, and actions that were created and see the pivot points that changed the directions for entire civilizations. For example, Western industrialized agriculture, dependent upon the development and use of chemicals and pesticides, was having a devastating impact on the global environment. It was a trend that almost nobody was aware of until the 1962 publication of Rachel Carson's *Silent Spring* documented the adverse environmental effects caused by indiscriminate use of pesticides. That one book single-handedly awakened the world to environmentalism and the importance of maintaining a healthy global ecosystem. In fact, the words "environmentalism" and "ecosystems" didn't exist before Carson's book came out.

Political, religious, and community systems experience their own emotional DNA, and they are subject to systemic principles and sentences and the same kind of limiting thinking as people are. And yet they, too, want to grow. I was hired by community leaders in a small town in the province of Quebec in Canada to do a constellations event. The town council wanted to get a handle on why the local economy continued to stagnate even though there was profound interest in developing the region. As we got into the first session, several of the local leaders said, "We must remember we are small."

"Where did that thought come from?" I asked.

"We have a saying here that goes, 'We're made for small bread,'" one of the leaders said. "We don't do big things."

There were other contributing factors, but that one limited, overarching sentence said it all about the emotional DNA of the region. How could the community possibly grow and evolve economically with a systemic sentence like that as their mantra?

Systemic Steppingstone #3:
A Quick Emotional DNA Check-In

What emotional DNA have you inherited? Are you the originator of an emotional DNA pattern? Ask yourself a few questions:

- Do you have a shared family language around a specific subject (e.g., relationships, money, work)?

- Do you have an emotional pattern that family members share (e.g., the men all feel diminished)?

- Do your family members have similar events, thoughts, and experiences in their lives (e.g., the women all leave)?

- Was there a particular event triggering an alignment with the way things are now (e.g., great-grandma left her "stupid" husband after he lost the family fortune, and now all the women marry men who don't do well with money, label them stupid, and then leave them)?

- Do you have an inner urging to do things differently from the usual family way?

- How long have you felt this way? Forever? Or did something trigger a desire for change?

- What was happening in your life at the time?

- What meaning did you create around this thought/feeling/pattern/situation?

- What did you make it mean about you and others?

CONSTELLATIONS

A constellation is a facilitated, three-dimensional process that enables you to see all parts of an issue and the spatial relationships among the components, along with the various origins and impacts of the issue. You can literally see, hear, touch, and explore parts of your system in real time. By engaging multiple senses and gaining new insights, you are able to stop the limiting cycles and access new possibilities.

A constellations event is usually held in a group setting. Clients take turns sharing and exploring their issue with the constellator (the facilitator). The constellator asks questions to gain an understanding of the scope and history of the issue. They then determine what parts of the issue need to be represented in the constellation—this may include system members, particular emotions like fear or anger, and even a specific event. The client chooses representatives from the other participants at the event to stand in for the various components of the issue. The client then physically places the representatives in spatial relationship to one another around the room in a way that reflects how the relationships and connections (or disconnections) seem to them.

It seems simple. But for most, it is the first time they have ever consciously looked at an issue or relationship in 3D. Now, here comes the fun part. Systems carry unique energies and information that can be quickly seen and then felt by both the client and representatives. Before the constellation begins, the representatives are asked to take a deep breath and exhale, letting go of their personal thoughts, ideas, and judgments so they can step into service of the client's system and be open and available to whatever information comes to them from the system. They are free to ask to speak or move—but only if they feel compelled to do so from a deeply felt, inner prompting, *not* from an intellectual headspace. The client is then invited to observe and pay close attention to the feelings, thoughts, and emotions they experience as the constellation unfolds. It isn't about role-playing, and it's not psychodrama. It is about the client and their system's representatives deeply connecting with the information field of the system known as "the knowing field" (which I explain in more detail in the next section of this chapter).

Here's an example of how a constellation works.

"Mom was never there for me," Rita said. "I've tried everything to get her to see me, but it's not happening."

"How does Mom being emotionally absent affect you?" I asked.

"I can't form intimate relationships. I'm really insecure and don't feel good enough about myself to do so." (Notice Rita has just told me that she, too, is emotionally absent in relationships. And she knows that somehow this is connected to her mom.)

"If your mom saw you, how would that make a difference?"

"If Mom saw me, I would know I'm good enough for others to see me."

At this point I asked Rita to select three event participants to physically represent her, her mother, and her father. I asked her if there had been any miscarriages, stillbirths, abortions, or children who had been adopted out. (Exclusions of any part of the system may cause confusion in the system.) She said there weren't, so I asked her to place each representative in spatial relationship to each other around the room.

How the client has spatially arranged all the representatives shows me things like who is connected or disconnected, who is close to someone or more distant from others, who is shut down or engaged. I ask questions about everything I notice. The first walk through the constellation is often quite illuminating for the client. They suddenly begin to *see, hear, and experience* the tensions and connections in relationships and the obstacles or possibilities between the system elements that they had never been able to figure out in their head. Patterns that have never been noticed before often emerge right in front of their eyes. In Rita's case, the representative for her mother just stood there looking down, and she continued to stare at the floor in front of her.

This kind of action can indicate that there's a missing member in the picture—a miscarriage or a child that died. I again asked Rita if her mom lost a child, and she looked perplexed, then gasped. "I forgot! She got pregnant right after I was born and lost the baby. She never had any more children after that."

We sat a representative for this missing child on the floor in front of "Mom." It was instantly clear to Rita why her mother never saw her. Her attention was on her lost baby.

"Do you understand why she might not be able to see you?" I asked.

"It's not about me at all!" Rita cried. "Oh my God! It wasn't me!"

So often as children we imagine that things are our fault, and we make up stories in our heads about how we aren't good enough in some way. Then we live our lives with those stories running the show when, truth is, often the situation had little to nothing to do with us.

For the very first time Rita was able to understand at a deep, gut level that her whole issue was about her mom's situation. The insight was enough to release the sense of diminished self that was ruining her life, and she was able to be more confident in relationships from that point on.

THE KNOWING FIELD

How did the representative for Rita's mother know to stand in the constellation staring at the floor? If asked, she most likely would have shrugged and said something like, "I don't know. I just felt compelled to do that."

Constellations facilitators describe the knowing field as a field of energy that holds all the information contained in the lives and events of the family system—a repository for every event, every thought, every feeling, every action, every inaction, everything that's happened within the system that goes back as far as we can imagine, forming clues and creating the wisdom of the ancients. We might call this "magic" because we don't fully understand it, but in logical reality, we all have access to ancient patterns. We just don't typically take the time to dimensionalize our relationships and inner world so we can see it. So we believe it doesn't exist when in fact it is alive and well and running our lives!

Participants who represent parts of a constellation frequently report changes in their perception and a clear sense of tapping into something other than themselves. Thousands of constellation sessions reveal that the feedback given by representatives about the people or situations they're representing is usually informative, illuminating, and startlingly accurate, providing the client with remarkable information, connections, and insights.

The client's senses are suddenly more focused as they become aware of parts of their system that they haven't consciously noticed or experienced before. Clients and representatives alike often begin to experience the same thoughts and feelings associated with the ones they are representing and the issue being explored. The client might say, "Wow, my stomach's hurting just the way it does when . . ." or "My heart's beating really fast just like when . . ." This is because a constellation is not just a flat, inert representation of an issue or whatever system you're exploring. It's a *dynamic* representation, and all the patterns and therefore energies of the family and issue itself are present.

As the representatives move and speak about what they are feeling, clients gain new insights into what is really in play. Often there is a shift for the representatives that creates yet another shift for the client, and that keeps happening until we reach a point where the movement and conversations stop and we can let the process rest, taking the insights that have been gained.

Unbelievable? Perhaps. We'll get into the actual science that validates the dynamics of the knowing field in the next chapter. In the meantime, here's a story about a highly skeptical and wealthy businessman who came to a constellation workshop and wound up representing a client's father, who was a Vietnam vet.

As a representative, he found himself feeling inexplicably ashamed and withdrawn. The client was deeply moved at how much he energetically resembled the father she'd grown up with. "When Dad came back from Vietnam, there were a lot of anti-war protests in our small town," she said. "As a vet, they singled him out and harassed him so badly we had to move. He was so ashamed and confused that he ended up withdrawing from us and life in general."

The businessman was unsettled by how deeply affected he was emotionally as a representative. When the client talked about her dad and affirmed his feelings of shame, he was plainly shocked. As we concluded the constellation, he started to cry. He revealed that his own father had dodged the draft for Vietnam and felt ashamed about it afterward. He'd never thought about it much until the constellation. Now he had insights from two points of view: the ashamed anti-war protestor and the shamed veteran who had served his country. He thanked the client for her father's service, and he put down the burden of his own father's guilt. But he remained deeply affected by the insights. Within the year he had created a scholarship for grandchildren of Vietnam vets.

ANCESTRAL HISTORY

It is impossible to convey the power and impact of a constellation. Clients often report sensing everything in more depth. Some say they can feel their body shifting and sense a mental shift occurring as their brains rewire. After their experience, clients often tell me, "I'm not thinking the same way anymore. I feel different," or "I no longer feel burdened." I remember a constellation where the client's issue was the same as Rita's—Amanda's mother never really seemed to see her or have time for her either. But this constellation played out quite differently.

Instead of looking at the floor, the representative for Amanda's mother stared fixedly outside the constellation. When I asked, "What happened to your mother?" Amanda replied that Grandma had no time for *her* daughter and that her mother and grandmother had never been close. So now I knew we had a pattern.

We placed representatives for her grandparents in the constellation. Sure enough, Amanda's "mom" turned to stare at her "mom," ignoring everyone else. In turn, the grandmother turned away and stared outside the circle, just like Amanda's mom had.

"What happened to your great-grandmother?" I asked.

She told me that her great-grandma was fine until her husband was killed, and then she had to work to put food on the table. She didn't have time to spend with any of her eight children, who suddenly had to depend upon each other for support. Bingo! That one insight revealed a multigenerational picture where all the women in her mother's line can't see their children. They're too busy looking for their own mothers and too busy taking care of other things.

"Do you have children?" I asked her.

"Yes, two daughters," she replied, tears in her eyes. "And there's a lot of tension between us. It's one of the reasons I came here today."

Imagine being the first woman in four generations to realize that a mother might be able to see her own daughter. Imagine realizing that you're changing a hundred-year, multigenerational pattern that was handed down to you. Imagine the empowerment of realizing that you aren't subject to fate, but rather have a destiny to create a different story.

We placed representatives for her great-grandparents in the constellation, and I asked Amanda to tell her great-grandmother that she saw her and understood what had happened. "Great-grandma, thank you for keeping us alive!" she said. "For you who didn't have time for all your children, watch me as I do it differently. Watch me see and engage with your great-great-grandchildren and bring back the connection and gentleness and fun that you didn't have time for."

With this simple act, understanding and respect replaced heartache and maternal distancing. As Amanda spoke to her great-grandmother, she was acknowledging what was, allowing healing to travel through her grandmother and mother while telling herself a profound new truth—that she would be there for her children, would see them and engage with them and play with them—allowing hope, passion, and purpose to travel forward through her lineage.

BEYOND INSIGHT LIES TRANSFORMATION

Often, the constellation process stops at issue resolution. Acknowledging what is—and that includes what has been—allows for movement to happen, which leads to resolution of an issue and a rewiring of the neurological network in our brains, creating a shift in our psychology and emotions.

The minute you can acknowledge "what is" exactly the way it is, without wishing for it to change, you are at ground zero. *Now* you can complete the pattern that is trying to end and start moving forward, because the past no longer has an unconscious hold on you.

But systemic work and constellations can take us far beyond resolution when we add one simple question: "What else is possible here?"

In my years of work with thousands of clients, I have realized that after resolution comes the possibility of transformation, and some clients are ready for a step in that direction. It has been my profound good fortune to realize that the pattern wanting to resolve and rest contains seeds for the new pattern that desires to be born through us. Moving beyond the space of feeling trapped, we begin to understand at a very deep level that we can be greater than what came before us, that nothing can ultimately trap or limit us, and that each of us can and should do something quite extraordinarily different with our lives. By using systemic work and constellations to see what is trying to emerge through us and to continue exploring our personal language and actions, we can keep growing, taking the gifts of the past and using them to fertilize and create the dreams of the future.

Systemic Steppingstone #4:
A Simple Constellation

To get a taste of what a constellation is all about, you can do a simple exercise at home using index cards, paper, or sticky notes.

Bringing a sense of curiosity and play into this process is helpful. If you're feeling resistant, remind yourself that you are here to grow your future, not repeat ancient history. Also, be aware that skeptical thinking ("This won't work for me!") is a meta pattern—a global human thought pattern that locks down most of humanity and keeps us from discovery and growth. Be present with this process and open to some new insights and wisdom!

- Write "Mom" on an index card (or whatever word you normally use).

- Write "Dad" on another card (or whatever word you normally use).

- Create a separate card for each sibling's name.

- Create cards for other prominent people in your life, such as coworkers, teachers, grandparents, uncles, aunts, chosen family members.

- Write your own name on a card.

Place the cards on the floor in an open area in any sort of arrangement that feels right to you and just notice:

- Are you in the middle? Are you on the outside?

- Who is close to you and who is farther away?

- Who is closest to whom?

- What does it feel like to see your "family" out in front of you like this?

- Stand on your own card and look around. What do you notice? What do you feel? Are any emotions coming up? Issues? Insights?

- Really take the time to listen to your thoughts and feel your feelings. The secret sauce to healing and transformation is learning to dialogue and interact with your inner world as effectively as your outer world, making the invisible visible.

CHAPTER 3

THE SCIENCE BEHIND SYSTEMIC WORK AND CONSTELLATIONS

Systemic work and constellations may seem startling in their effectiveness, even disturbingly uncanny, but there are many credible, scientific explanations from the fields of neuroscience, epigenetics, quantum physics, and psychoneuroimmunology (the study of the relationship between your central nervous system and immune system) backing up what's happening. Some of the science presented in this chapter is advanced theory and has yet to be proven. Some of it is still hypothesis. Most of it is wildly cutting edge. But, then, so is systemic work and constellations.

As the famous American science fiction writer Arthur C. Clarke once said: "Any sufficiently advanced technology is indistinguishable from magic."[1]

Now, let's take a look at the dynamics of constellations from a scientific perspective and see how it actually works.

> Question: How can doing a constellation shift my perception of the world, enabling me to operate as a whole new person?

> Short answer: Neuroscience

American psychiatrist Dr. Milton Erickson once said, "If you want happiness, you have to work for it."[2] And he was right. Happiness in life isn't automatic or guaranteed. But no matter what the past has brought us, the possibility for creating the world we want, including happiness, begins with us.

Until recently, doctors and researchers believed that the human brain was "hardwired" by the time we were in our twenties—that our thoughts and beliefs were difficult, if not impossible, to change after that, and that we inevitably became more inflexible as we got older. And yet, as far back as the early twentieth century, the "father of neuroscience," Santiago Ramón y Cajal, described nonpathological changes in the neuronal structure of adult brains as "neuronal plasticity."[3] In 1949, the Canadian psychologist Donald Hebb studied how neurons in the brain adapt during learning. He talked about how new neuronal patterns in the brain are developed through association, famously saying, "Neurons wire together if they fire together."[4]

By the time the 1960s came along, the term "neuroplasticity" had come into vogue, but the age-old belief that adult brains are unchanging prevailed in the mainstream until the end of the century. Fortunately, researchers like American psychiatrist Norman Doidge, MD, author of the book *The Brain That Changes Itself: Stories of Personal Triumph from the Frontiers of Brain Science,* have finally helped us change our minds. "The brain can change itself," writes Doidge. "It is a plastic, living organ that can actually change its own structure and function, even into old age."[5]

The vision of a living, changing brain that responds to new experiences throughout one's lifespan is most certainly a vision of hope. Studies now show that new neural pathways can be formed or reprogrammed over a period of about twenty-one days, with the new behavior becoming automatic within sixty-six days on average.[6]

And yet most people live on autopilot most of their lives, changing very little. This is, to a great extent, because our neural pathways operate under the law of least effort or the path of least resistance, allowing us to conserve mental energy and respond quickly to life experiences.

Let's say you were bitten by a dog when you were five years old. Thoughts that have a strong emotion attached to them, like fear, create neural pathways very quickly. During traumatic or highly significant events, we are flooded with a ton of data that leads our brains to operate in survival or hyper-perceptive mode, activating neural networks at speed. If a situation is intense enough or is repeated enough times without resolution, we start laying down neural pathways that are amplified by the emotions in play. Which means that after the traumatic dog bite experience, you rapidly develop a generalized fear of dogs. You get frightened every time a dog is present, and the biochemicals triggered by the fear reinforce the mental program "dogs are dangerous" over and over again. Soon the brain creates a deeply ingrained, habitual response pathway that kicks in quickly and efficiently every time you see a dog.

The same is true of everything else in life. We quickly develop mental habits and think the same thoughts over and over about certain people, situations, ideas, and beliefs. By the time we're in our twenties, we don't have to really think at all. We just follow the same old neural cow paths in our brains, thinking the same thoughts about politics and religion, our parents, money, our next-door neighbor, our ex-spouse, and on and on. If we don't complete or close out these patterns in a way that settles our brain, then thoughts about these ideas, people, and events constantly fire and neurologically wire the same pattern with the same physical and emotional responses.

Habitual mental patterns and multigenerational fears and responses that repeat over and over again can result in PTSD, flashbacks, nightmares, illnesses, and other conditions. The brain can become so hair-trigger primed that even the faintest suggestion of that pathway can cause us to be triggered—for example, there can be a fear response to a picture of a dog. This pattern can then be passed down through the generations as a pattern of thoughts, feelings, and actions via something called epigenetics, which we will discuss shortly. Systemic sentences are also created, like: "We're not dog people." Or "Everyone in my family has depression." Or "We are all overweight/angry/poor." Or "We don't borrow money." Or "We would rather die than betray our values."

Fortunately, neuroplasticity guarantees we can change our neural pathways, and during a constellation, our neural pathways can change very rapidly. "Family constellations may actively involve the ability of the brain to rewire itself through new sensory experiences, thereby creating new neural pathways," says Yildiz Sethi, psychotherapist and founder of Rapid Core Healing and Emotional Mind Integration. "Hence, providing the space for a new story to emerge of victory over the odds, surviving, or better still thriving, rather than remaining a victim of circumstance."[7]

During a constellation, we identify the issue and its components and approach the work with a curious, open, inquiring, and present state of mind that tends to create the space for possibility, deepening awareness and generating more insights. But the most impactful aspect of a constellation is its 3D nature. Physically experiencing the spatial representation of the family constellation (or business or organizational constellation) that the client has set up creates a shift in perception, as they now see and hear and sense the constellation's patterns for the first time.

Here's a story of a client I worked with during a constellations event that shows what I mean.

Sandra couldn't find her place at work or at home and always felt excluded. She was the "different one" in the family and often skipped out on family gatherings because she felt like she wasn't wanted. This same dynamic was beginning to show up at work, where she would remove herself from teams and then wonder why she was being excluded from business gatherings. Of course, the truth was she was the one excluding herself from both private and work engagements, but she just couldn't see it.

When she was turned down for a promotion after receiving feedback that her distancing made others uncomfortable, Sandra knew it was time to look at what was holding her back. I asked her to pick a representative for her mother, father, and siblings and a representative for herself, and to set them up in a spatial relationship to one another in the way that felt right to her.

As she picked and placed her representatives, I noticed that they all kept looking around as though they were searching for someone. I asked Sandra if somebody was missing, and if so, who that might be. She didn't know, so I tested by placing a representative in the spot that all the other representatives kept looking at. Everyone in the constellation focused on the newcomer, and Sandra's representative actually moved to stand right next to her.

The new "unknown" representative stood still for a while, then walked out of the circle and over to some bottles of water. She grabbed a few and moved back to her spot, and for the next few minutes didn't look up or make eye contact with any of the other representatives. She did, however, open the bottles of water and drink and drink and drink. With each bottle her head drooped lower. After drinking four bottles of water, she started to edge away from the group.

Sandra stared at her and then started to cry. "I know who it is," she said, tears running down her face. "My mom's mom was never the same after her husband was killed. Mom said she just wanted to die with him. She started avoiding family members and family gatherings and began drinking heavily. She disappeared one night after a drinking binge. They found her in a ditch, days later. Nobody spoke about her or Grandfather much because it was just too painful."

I asked Sandra if she could tell her grandmother's representative, "I see you, and I see that I exclude myself just like you did." Then I asked if she could give her grandmother a place in her heart and maybe put a picture of her in her home. Sandra nodded, wiping the tears from her cheeks, and cried, "I don't want to disappear like she did!"

At that point, the representative for the grandmother put down the last bottle of water she was holding and stared at a point outside of the circle. (Often, a representative who moves outside of the circle has a wish to leave the "circle of life.") When I placed a representative for her husband where she was looking, she moved over to where he was standing outside the circle of life and settled right down. In a moment of revelation and closure, Sandra walked up to her "grandmother" and said, "I see you, and I see how painful this was for you. For you who couldn't stay with the family and belong, I can. I will always have a place for you. Thank you for showing me what this cost you. Your heart closed and it killed you. Watch me as I open mine and live a full life."

Sandra described the moment to the group later. "It felt as though a huge weight had been lifted off my shoulders. Suddenly, I felt like I could belong in ways I hadn't for a long time." Within a year of the event, she bypassed the original promotion she had wanted and was given a large team to work with because of her ability to pull people together and create belonging. A year after the promotion, she met and found the love of her life.

A picture of her grandmother and grandfather hangs in her hallway to this day.

In terms of neurological rewiring, when Sandra walked through her family constellation and saw all the representatives looking outside the constellation, obviously searching for someone missing, she *physically* experienced the truth that someone was absent . . . a perception she hadn't been able to reach simply by thinking about her family because her brain's neurological network was fixed in the old pattern that excluded her grandmother and grandfather.

When she saw her "grandmother" drinking and moving away from the constellation, it hit her viscerally. Her inherited pattern was right there, clearly visible for the first time. It was like being doused with a bucket of cold water—surprising and astonishing—and the emotion that accompanied this instant shift in perception created a cascade of biochemicals in her body and brain that ensured that her new view was *instantly* being wired deeply into her brain and consciousness. The new insight into her own life was so powerful, it was impossible for her to ignore or forget. At that point, her perception of her entire history and future began to shift.

It is precisely the visceral, experiential power of constellations work that makes neurological rewiring and change possible. You engage multiple senses. You see and hear and sense something you haven't perceived before, your brain starts making new neurological connections, the intense feelings and emotions cement the shift, and a totally new perception and reality begins to take hold.

Systemic Steppingstone #5:
The Twenty-One-Day Challenge

Take the twenty-one-day challenge and create your own scientific experiment! Lay down a conscious neural pathway and notice the difference. Pick one behavior or thought pattern that you would like to change and commit completely to shifting it. No ifs, ands, buts, or excuses. Your clear intention is to make that twenty-one-day challenge! Now write down one new thought. Notice one new feeling. State the new thought out loud until you feel it take hold and you give it your full-on "Yes!" If you can tie the new thought and feelings to a goal, so much the better. Remember, elevated emotions are the fuel that sustains you.

Question: How is it possible to express the traits, habits, and thoughts of my ancestors?

Short answer: Epigenetics

There is a popular saying in systemic work that goes: "When you fail to do your own work, you leave it to your children to pick up and repeat the incompletions you won't address." In the last chapter, I said that you don't just inherit your physical DNA, you also inherit your patterns of thoughts, feelings, actions, and reactions. Epigenetics—the study of how events, choices, behaviors, and environmental conditions cause changes that affect the way our genes work, affecting generations beyond the originally impacted member—is a likely candidate for explaining this phenomenon.

Our genetic code creates proteins in a process called gene expression. Genetic changes alter which proteins are made and thus which genes are expressed. Epigenetic changes triggered by environmental factors don't alter the proteins produced or change the genetic code. They do, however, create "marks" that turn certain genes "on" and "off." Unlike genetic changes, epigenetic changes are reversible and do not change your DNA sequence. But they do affect how your body *reads* and then expresses a DNA sequence.

Burgeoning studies indicate that external factors such as diet and exercise, trauma, emotional stress, and other physical and psychological effects can result in epigenetic changes that can be passed down to subsequent generations. For example, rats exposed to prenatal stress, maternal separation, abusive caregiving, and adult social stress show epigenetic changes in their DNA. There is also evidence that abusive caregiving traits are passed down to both offspring and grand-offspring.[8]

Studies of children of Holocaust survivors have revealed that the trauma their ancestors experienced may have left a chemical mark on their genes that was passed down, resulting in higher anxiety levels, lower self-esteem, greater inhibition of aggression, and more relational difficulties than those found in control groups.[9]

One of the more well-documented epigenetic studies was conducted on pregnant mothers during the great Dutch Hunger Winter between November 1944 and May 1945.[10] Toward the end of World War II, the western Netherlands was punished for working with the Allies by a blockade set up by the Germans. The general population resorted to eating rats, grass, and tulip bulbs to survive.

Pregnant women who were malnourished during the early stages of pregnancy demonstrated higher rates of obesity, mental health issues, and other health problems later in life. Significantly, some of these effects were still present in the *grandchildren*. The epigenetic environmental markers were passed down, and the phenotype—the observable characteristics of an individual resulting from the interaction of its genotype with the environment—was inherited.

Epigenetic markers appear as patterns of thoughts, feelings, language, actions, and reactions. I see them in the ancestral patterns that clients repeat in many areas, including relationships, success, purpose, fears, dreams, finances, leadership, and health. I hear these markers in the unique and often idiosyncratic language that clients speak—unwritten yet clearly understood rules that run the family systems of which they are a part.

Here the ideas of nature and nurture come together. We have the genes we've inherited from our parents, but *how* they express depends on what's around us, how we are nurtured and, most importantly, the meaning *we* have made of what surrounds and affects us. Over time the details of events fade, but their symptoms get louder and louder until what needs to be noticed in the system is seen and resolved.

Epigenetic effects can be changed. When clients intentionally rewire their patterns of thoughts, feelings, and actions, their brains and their reality are literally no longer the same . . . and neither is their ancient history or hitherto predictable future. When you finally recognize old family patterns, the door to the remarkable opens and you are able to generate, experience, and embody an evolutionary leap.

Question: How does a representative pick up information from the client and the knowing field?

Short answer: Morphic resonance, quantum mechanics, intention, and the holographic universe

Morphic Resonance

Rupert Sheldrake, PhD, author and former developmental biologist at Cambridge University in the UK, developed a theory called morphic resonance, a process whereby self-organizing systems inherit a memory from previous similar systems. Sheldrake believes that social fields, including human fields, have a kind of social memory (perhaps what Swiss psychoanalyst Carl Jung called the collective unconscious). Echoes of actions, words, thoughts, and feelings form what Sheldrake refers to as laws or habits. He says that families have fields and that patterns and habits exist within them, something that is well documented in systemic work and constellations.

Fields are related to information. For example, in psychology, Field Theory recognizes and examines the patterns created between an individual and the total field of their environment. In classical physics, electromagnetic (EM) fields are created by moving electrical charges. The human body, which is electrical in nature, produces an EM field. Our bodies constantly receive EM radiation from the Earth's field and the fields of other human beings and animals. Our eyes intercept electromagnetic radiation in the visible light spectrum from objects and interpret it. Studies show that human beings can detect the Earth's EM field (mostly unconsciously) and actually transform it in the brain.[11] There is even speculation in scientific and technological circles on whether each person's EM field is unique and whether or not we can create devices that can eventually "read" a person's EM signature like a fingerprint or retinal scan.

Anybody who has had the experience of sensing another person's presence and instantly knowing who it was before actually seeing or hearing them just might be tapping into their EM signature.

Sheldrake speculates that through morphic resonance, the occurrence of events in one place creates similar events in other places, perhaps generations apart.[12] The knowing field may thus be a repository of events and all the decisions and actions that occurred around those events, made available for exploration in the present moment. Morphic resonance also supports the possibility that when a child is born, an entire field of knowledge experienced by earlier ancestors is available to the child—not because the information was passed down epigenetically, but because the genetics of the child resonate to the genetics of his or her predecessors that carry the old repository of information.

Quantum Mechanics, Intention, and Entanglement

Prior to 1905, the physical universe could be explained by Newtonian physics. Atoms were pictured as tiny solid planets zipping through space, and the tiny physical particles that made up atoms, forming the foundation of matter, were thought to be concrete objects. Then Einstein came along and taught us that matter is actually energy ($E = mc^2$) and suddenly all bets were off. Electron microscopes proved that atoms were made up of "particles" that had electrical charge but no mass whatsoever. Apparently, every "thing" in the world, including the world itself, is made up of formless energy.

Einstein also explained the photoelectric effect, theorizing that instead of waves, light came in discrete packets of "energy quanta," later to be called photons. Then it was discovered that light exhibits the properties of both a wave and a particle *simultaneously*, and something called the double slit experiment introduced an astounding element into the world of quantum physics: *consciousness*.

Experiments showed that the act of measuring and observing determined whether a photon showed up as an energy packet (also referred to as a particle) or as a wave. In 1920, physicist Niels Bohr came up with an explanation for this puzzling phenomenon in the Copenhagen interpretation, proposing that *the act of observing the experiment changes the outcome*.[13] Consciousness apparently affects the quantum field . . . which means the thoughts of the client may be subtly influencing the representatives and the knowing field during a constellation.

Although it is still highly controversial and not conclusively proven, studies also show that mental intention does interact with the energetic quantum field that underlies all of reality. In the early 1960s, experiments by Canadian psychologist Bernard Grad showed that seeds irrigated with water held by a healer germinated and grew faster than controls.[14] Intrigued by these early studies, since June 2007, investigative journalist and author Lynne McTaggart has set up six similar Germination Intention Experiments to determine if intention could have a quantifiable effect on living systems. Consistently, in all six experiments, seeds that were sent intention grew taller than the controls.[15]

This is why it is paramount that, in constellations, the facilitator have no expectations and intentions influencing the client and coloring the experience within the constellation. The existence of the quantum field and the potential impact of intention is one of the major reasons the facilitator must remain neutral.

Another mysterious aspect of quantum mechanics that might help explain constellations is entanglement. Experiments have proven that when two electrons come in contact with each other, their spin states become linked. They bump into one another and, from that moment on, if the spin state of one of those electrons changes, the spin state of the other electron changes to match it *instantaneously*, even if the two electrons are a million light years apart. It's like one kiss and they're married forever.

In a knock-out punch, the double slit experiment obliterated the most trusted belief in thousands of years of science: the idea that the scientist is totally objective and separate from the world they are studying. Entanglement proved everything in the universe is fundamentally connected at an energetic level. If the basic elements of the universe are all interconnected in an infinite, entangled web, and if human consciousness can affect that web, the world we think we know so well is not at all what it seems.

The Holographic Universe

The theory that the universe is actually a gigantic hologram has been kicking around the scientific world since the early 1990s. In 2017, researchers published findings in the journal *Physical Review Letters* providing substantial evidence that we are indeed living in a two-dimensional universe that looks three dimensional.[16] But what's interesting here is the quirky nature of a hologram itself.

Remember the holographic projection of Princess Leia pleading, "Help me, Obi-Wan Kenobi. You're our only hope!" way back in 1977 in the movie *Star Wars*? If we take a single pixel from one frame of that holographic image (let's say one pixel from Princess Leia's dress) and examine that pixel, what we'd expect to see is a pixel of a piece of cloth. Right? But, according to the holographic theory, what you will actually see is the entire holographic image of Princess Leia. The nature of a hologram is such that the whole holographic image is found in every fragment of the image. The many is contained in the One—a mystical concept found in many esoteric teachings of the major religions describing the nature of the universe. Which means all the systemic information in the morphogenic field of the constellation is available to everyone in the room.

SCIENCE SUMMARY

Now we potentially have all the background information needed to answer the questions of how a constellation works, how Sandra carries ancestral information, how the representative for Sandra's grandmother knew to pick up those water bottles, drink, and then leave the constellation, and how the insight this triggered instantly changed Sandra's reality forever. Ready?

1. Neuroscience = an explanation for how Sandra can experience an instantaneous shift in perception during the constellation, interrupting old patterns of thought, changing her personal reality forever.

2. Epigenetics + morphogenic field theory = an explanation for Sandra carrying ancestral patterns of thought and action into her present-day experience and into the constellation.

3. $E = mc^2$ + entanglement + the holographic universe = the answer to how the constellation (the knowing field) is created. It is composed of entangled fields of quantum energy and information, including the information of Sandra's family system.

4. $E = mc^2$ + entanglement + the holographic universe + intention = Sandra's discovery of healing information via the impact of her intention on the quantum field, interconnecting everything in the constellation and setting the stage for answers to appear.

5. Morphogenic fields + $E = mc^2$ + intention + entanglement = the representative for Sandra's grandmother "knowing" to drink water and then leave the constellation.

Over the years, I've conducted thousands of constellations and witnessed thousands of breakthroughs and innumerable breathtaking "aha" moments. I've seen people's lives dramatically change in the space of a few heartbeats. I've watched this transformation happen over and over again. Now, you've just been given some of the best scientific explanations currently available on how it works. Whether or not these explanations are accurate only time and more research will tell.

Systemic Steppingstone #6:
Experiencing the Science and the Field

The best way to help pull all the information in this chapter together is to experience what you've read about. And the best way to do that is to do a constellation.

In Systemic Steppingstone #4, I invited you to step into and see your family system. Now you are going to do the same using any of your other systems or issues—perhaps you want to explore a business relationship or take a look at a specific issue or task at work that has you stuck or pondering.

Identify all the relevant components of the system you wish to see, interact with, and explore. Lay the pieces out the way that feels right to you without overthinking it. Again, use the floor or a tabletop for your system layout. See, touch, and rearrange those pieces, noticing the relationships between each component. *Feel* who is engaged or not. *Sense* the relationships between the components/people.

This is you "reading" the field, sensing the invisible quantum information that lies within it. This is what great leaders are talking about when they talk about following their gut or their heart. They sense what's going on around them in a way that transcends mere physical evidence, their hearts are opened, and their minds are inspired to create at a whole new level.

CHAPTER 4

PRACTICAL MAGIC (AKA TRANSFORMATION)

We tend to classify as "magic" something that happens in an instant and that afterward leaves us scratching our heads, wondering, "How'd that happen?" The inexplicable nature of magic catches our attention and invokes a sense of wonder. Something incredibly lovely happens—something new pops up in front of us, prompting an insight that makes us smile and grow—we take a yellow crayon and scribble over the blue sky we just colored, and instead of a mess, out comes a green sky. Amazing!

This is what life is really like when we are truly awake to it. In an instant, things can change, and a whole new sky can present itself. But we tend to get locked into patterns of thoughts, feelings, and beliefs where transformation doesn't seem possible. We think the sky can only be blue. We think we're not supposed to color outside the lines or mix colors. We're afraid of doing things wrong or differently. Even though both blue and yellow sit in our box of crayons, we miss the magic of creating green.

And yet we yearn for more—more colors to play with, more opportunities, more abilities, more freedom. We yearn to be greater, and the entertainment industry knows this very well, continually feeding us worlds filled with magic and adventure: *Star Wars*, *Once*, *Bewitched*, *The Magicians*, *Merlin*, *Harry Potter* . . . the list is endless. We know an incredible part of us exists, but we can't seem to find our way into it like our fictional heroes do. We wait for a magical moment on a mountainside, a lightning bolt from the sky, an alien encounter in the middle of a corn field. We keep looking *out there* instead of *in here*.

We forget that magic begins and ends in our own hearts. We don't expect to find magic in ourselves and the events of our daily lives, let alone our multigenerational history that is trying so hard to speak to us. What could possibly be magical about that? And when we do experience something amazing, we quickly find a way to label the moment as coincidental or lucky.

We long for magic but have been taught to fear it. Somewhere, a long time ago, the word "magic" took on overtones of "the Devil's work" at worst, pure silliness and wishful thinking at best. Superstitious fears swung our focus firmly away from much that is wonderful and surprising both in nature and in us. Many of the incredible scientific theories explored in the last chapter continue to be labeled "ridiculous," not because there isn't strong supporting scientific evidence, but because in our fear and skepticism we think, "That just can't be possible. It can't be that outrageous and easy!"

And then there's the fact that for hundreds of years many global religions have trained us to believe we are worthless sinners. We've come to believe that living incredible, joyful lives is not only unattainable but undeserved and even something to be feared. A huge global, systemic sentence of "I am nothing and unworthy" prevails and runs much of the world, and it serves no one.

Being big isn't boastful and aggressive. The biggest people I know are wonderful women and men who show others what's possible. They encourage people around them to go for greatness because they know it's possible. They know the indescribable bliss of stepping beyond predetermined limits and fear, and they want others to share in the experience. They know that transformation isn't a wishful idea or a New Age woo-woo hypothesis. It's a sort of practical magic. They know the bigger version of themselves is inside them, waiting to be actualized.

Just like George. George was disillusioned and cynical and, as he put it, had the presence and curiosity of an exceedingly small mouse. For as long as he could remember, he'd had no joy. He knew it was his duty to do well and be a good citizen, but happiness wasn't on his agenda. Over the years he'd been to many transformative events that made him feel good for about an hour, and then he quickly reverted to the same old feeling of blah.

Told about systemic work and constellations, he came to an event, reluctantly curious. He endured the theory and information at the beginning and challenged everything he heard. By lunch, he was convinced this was another dead end.

When we did the first constellation, Lily shared about her painfully distant relationship with her brother in an emotional way that made George cringe. But he was mildly intrigued by the direction of the questions being asked. When we set up the constellation, to his shock, Lily asked him to represent her brother. He didn't do emotions and touchy-feely things and almost excused himself, but it was too late. Reluctantly he entered the constellation, allowing Lily to place him facing outward toward a window.

"Why is your brother facing away?" I asked.

"We used to be close. But he's been gone from the family for a long time," she replied. "Ever since he went on a tour of duty overseas, he hasn't been the same."

Listening to this, George felt his throat tighten, and his hands began to shake. For once in his life, instead of analyzing things to death, he allowed himself to just sink into the feelings that were washing over him—feelings he hadn't experienced before.

I asked him what he was feeling.

"I feel a sense of dread and fear building in my stomach and chest," he said. Then he pointed in front of him.

A new representative was placed where he indicated, and he found himself pointing to more and more empty spaces. As each one filled with a new representative, he found himself drawn to move outside the circle to where the representatives were standing. When I asked him if he could come back, he shook his head, moving closer to where the others were standing. "I belong here," he said.

Lily burst into tears.

In cases of war, there are many incompletions. Conversations not had, fellow soldiers left behind, friends' lives lost in combat. War forms a system of its own, and when soldiers return home to a set of rules that are in conflict with the rules of engagement and war, they can be caught between two systems. What is expected in war is not allowed in civilian life. The ugliness of war is excluded from view and acknowledgment. Unless what's happened to returning soldiers is addressed and given its place, unless their yearning for completion with lost buddies is satisfied, returning soldiers can become lost. It's not that they don't see their children or family members. It's just that their focus is still "over there."

For Lily, just this one insight was enough. Seeing a representation of what was going on for her brother, suddenly she didn't feel so alienated. She could do something. She could talk to her brother in an entirely different way. Standing in the constellation, she reported that her thoughts had immediately switched from, "There's nothing I can do. I'm a bad sister," to "It's not my fault. It's not that he's left us. It's that he hasn't found his way back yet." She reported feeling a huge weight being lifted off her shoulders and an immediate sense of calm settling in.

George, however, was an entirely different story. Later he said, "The dam burst, and there was no stopping it." He sobbed for a long time, feeling as though he wasn't just crying for himself but for many, many others. Turns out his father was a war vet who had gone out a happy man and returned without any happiness left. He'd seen a lot of action, and when he returned home, he slept in his own room, and often there were shouts at night when his father had nightmares. "There were no Christmases or birthday celebrations," he said. "My father said too many people on both sides lost their lives and there was nothing to be joyful about. He taught me it was my duty to be a good citizen, to work hard and take care of others. But happiness was off the table."

In the constellation that day, George realized he'd been so desperate to have his father see him, even just a little, that he'd obeyed the "no joy" orders without exception. Now his father was in a nursing home with Alzheimer's, and George had lost his purpose in life. He'd done well for himself financially but didn't know what to do with his wealth other than plod along, joylessly taking care of others.

As we spoke, I wondered what might happen if we placed representatives for George, his father, and joy in the circle, just to see what would happen. The room was quiet, and George was hesitant, but he agreed. Inviting the representatives to move if they needed to, George's "father" moved out of the circle and faced away. Joy followed him but stopped at the edge of the circle. After a while joy turned around and looked at George's representative. I invited George to replace his representative.

George stood for the longest time looking at his father. "I can't do this anymore," he finally said, choking up. "I see what happened to my dad, and I'm turning into more of that." He wiped away the tears and waited until he could speak. "I think I'd really like to bring joy back into my life. I'd like to bring smiles to people's faces, see them, and be joyful in my own heart. I know my father couldn't do it any differently, but I can."

Boom! Transformation! George flipped the script for himself right there. He could see that his father wouldn't have wished this joyless life for him and said "Yes" to something new without excluding or denying what had happened. Having experienced another possibility through the constellation, George's heart opened. He understood that joyless duty had been a form of love and connection to his father, but now he wanted to honor him in a different way. He could choose a different reality and allow it to grow. He said "Yes" without resistance, and his life changed.

He later reported back that he had set up scholarships for children who had lost a parent to war, presenting them with the story about his own father, giving them the opportunity to experience the gift of understanding and joy as well. "I love seeing the smiles on their faces when they get that they can be joyful," he said.

WE ARE MAGICIANS AND WIZARDS

We truly are wizards and magicians. We cast "spells" every single day with the words we use, the beliefs we hold onto, the thoughts we think, the feelings we feel, and the meanings we make out of the events in our lives. "Spells" is just another word for patterns, mindsets, and the truths we create. And the people we're casting spells upon are ourselves and those around us.

My client Alix simply could not feel good. She constantly felt "off," scared, and unsure of herself. Many times she told me she didn't know if she would be okay. One day, I asked her when those words had begun for her. She thought for a bit and her eyes widened. "The day I was told that my father had a terminal illness, I turned around to my line manager and said: 'I am not going to be okay.'"

She said it, she felt it, and she made it her truth. She cast a systemic spell and swallowed it. And it happened to her in a split second. After that, every time she was sad or something went wrong, she reinforced her declaration, and the power of the thought of not being okay built and built. Life no longer felt rich or exciting. She was not okay.

We looked at all the things she had accomplished and never enjoyed because of that sentence. Then I asked her if "not okay" was really the truth for her right now. To her surprise, she realized the sentence no longer fit. She took a long walk and talked out loud to her late father, letting him know how okay she was, thanking him for being there for her growing up. She said, "You empowered me to accomplish so much, and when you died, a part of me wanted to die too. Now it's time you knew that I'm okay."

Alix broke the spell of the mindset she had created and invested in so heavily. With her newfound peace and a new sentence of "I am doing well, and I am okay," she felt a heaviness leave her heart that was instantly replaced by a sense of freedom and joy she hadn't felt since he died.

Spells can lock us down so tightly we can't move. Spells can boost us so far into the stratosphere that our heads spin in delight. As spell makers, we need to realize our power and constantly reflect upon our thoughts and actions. "Am I creating heaven or hell with this thought?" is a good question to keep asking yourself.

Systemic Steppingstone #7: Discovering Your Body's Compass

As you will discover throughout this book, your body is an accurate compass pointing you toward your personal truth. It's been telling you all sorts of things throughout your life about yourself and your systems via your thoughts, beliefs, actions, reactions, feelings, ill health, and symptoms.

Here's a quick way to experience your body's compass and the difference between the outdated patterns (a limiting "spell") and the ones trying emerge through you (a possibility "spell"). Get out two pieces of paper. On one write down something you think you *should* do. On the other write down something you are *yearning* to do.

Place one paper at one end of a room and the other at the opposite end. Stand between the two pieces of paper and tune in to what you feel. Which way are you pulled? What are the voices in your head telling you about each one? Try moving closer to each piece of paper, and as you do, notice what you feel and where in your body you feel it. Is it a familiar feeling? What do you tell yourself about it? When did this feeling first start? Pay attention to what you hear. What are those voices saying? How do they make you feel?

When you find yourself feeling joyful and happy or filled with gratitude, you know you're pointed in the right direction. Ask yourself, "How might my life change if I invested fully in this?"

CREATING THROUGH JOY, GRATITUDE, AND EXCITEMENT

The magic of your transformation is very cleverly hidden in plain sight. It begins in your family and other systems and expresses through your pain points, dislikes, and likes. All you have to do is realize that the pain and dislikes are old patterns that have outlived their usefulness. They're asking you to set them down, release the "spell," and begin to use them as sources of wisdom. Then, look at what you like and desire. That suitcase full of dreams of yours is packed to the hilt with potential; it's just waiting for you to choose it and run with it. Your dreams and desires and all the things you yearn for are where the gold has been hidden all along. Systems need you to *want* and imagine the future. It's how they thrive and grow.

You are the dream maker.

When I want to accomplish or experience something that brings me joy and fulfillment, I am filled with an absolute sense of excitement and adventure. In this elevated emotional state, I allow myself to vividly imagine having what I want. I *feel* and sense how it is to be that person having and doing what excites me. I relax. *I don't look at the practicalities and obstacles.* I allow myself to have an adventure of imagination, placing myself squarely in the new space, trying my creation on for size, just like I would a new set of clothes.

If I really, really like what I've created, *then* I start looking for the smallest step I can take toward experiencing that. Often, it's a sentence or an insight or a feeling of joy and anticipation. With an internal mini-adventure brewing, I feel happier and more grateful. And the more grateful I feel, the more I feed that sense of gratitude, the closer my desire moves toward reality. Plainly put—I now have direction, purpose, and increasingly positive motivation.

So-called daydreaming, also known as creative meditation, is the key to discovering what you want to experience and bring into manifestation. You are not wasting time. You are consciously investing in yourself and your dream, and doing it with an attitude of relaxed enjoyment. Play is essential here because it doesn't alert your mind to stir up all the logical reasons why you might not be able to have what you want. It lowers resistance.

When I get clear on what I am dreaming into existence, I become super aware of any thoughts or feelings or resistance that might limit me, and I immediately begin to change or attend to those. I name them. I write them down and place them on the floor so I can interact with them, feel them, see what they have to say, and resolve any incompletions so that I can shift. I do the exercises presented in this book. I look at where the limiting piece may have started and remind myself that I can change that *now*. It's what I was born to do. *Me!* I am the magician using creativity to grow and transform. The more I love what I am creating, the more I am teaching myself what I can achieve and the closer I am getting to my dream.

Systemic Steppingstone #8: Playful, Creative Meditation

Okay, time to have some fun! Turn off the phone, find a place to relax without being interrupted, and spend some time playing with a dream—something that really jazzes you to the max. Something you've always wanted to do or have or be. *Don't limit yourself.* You'll know when you've hit on the right thing because you'll feel excitement

building in your body. You'll feel a sense of joy and fulfillment. Maybe your mouth will water!

Dive in. Be outrageous. Don't hold back. But above all,
get the felt sense of you being that version of yourself. Bask
in the feelings that course through you. Allow them in fully.
Follow them and see where they lead . . . the pictures that
form for you. If something catches your attention and says
"Yes!" remember that picture and that feeling. Create a clear
picture and feeling of you in that dream. You are creating a
new reality that is out of the old systemic pattern and part
of the new you, moving beyond the don'ts and can'ts. That
is how you wire in new realities and create new emotional
DNA. Do this for twenty-one days and see what unfolds
for you.

PART II

FOLLOWING
THE CLUES

CHAPTER 5

UNCOVERING THE HIDDEN GEMS

Symptoms Are Gold Mines

We use and create patterns as a way to navigate life. Maybe your mother is constantly saying, "Nobody likes a loudmouth." You speak out of turn one time and get seriously shut down, and you decide your mother was right. From then on, you unconsciously or consciously accept that it's dangerous to speak out and that "nice people keep quiet." As an adult, you might have great knowledge worthy of sharing, but because you've adopted the pattern of being well mannered and quiet, to be safe, you remain silent.

This pattern may work for you for quite a while. You might even become known as the quiet, deep, thoughtful one. You might even wear it as a badge of honor or tell yourself, "Nobody gets me." You may find yourself resentful or disdainful of people's shallowness and experience increasing frustration that your wisdom remains unshared.

Bear in mind, this habit may have begun generations ago with a vocal ancestor who was shut down—possibly excluded for *their* views. Who knows? They rightfully passed on words of caution around speaking up, but now you are still reacting to an ancient pattern that's been shared by the generations right down to your mother and then swallowed by you. I am constantly telling clients that, over time, the details of events fade, but the symptoms get louder and louder until they are seen, resolved, and integrated.

A frightening period of enforced quiet and a learned practice of keeping a low profile during the Nazi occupation in order to avoid capture and deportation to a concentration camp is one thing. Two generations later, the pattern of heightened self-effacement is no longer needed. It is a hindrance, and your loyalty to your pattern keeps you from living a full and wonderful life. As renowned systemic coach Anton de Kroon put it, "For what was this problem first a solution?"

Over the course of the next few chapters, we're going to explore the two categories of patterns in your life that sit side by side: the pattern that wants to rest and the pattern that wants to emerge. Each is in service to the other. Chances are one or the other is active in your day-to-day living. The pattern that wants to rest informs and ignites you through various symptoms, and the pattern that wants to emerge helps you pivot and create the new.

NOTICE THE SYMPTOMS

Limiting issues are often a powerful and helpful sign that something new is needed. There is a pattern in you that is trying to rest. Its usefulness has shifted from being an active pattern of protection to a pattern of learned limitation. You've been quiet all your life, and now something in you is bursting to come out. Your irritation and anger with others speaking out isn't wrong. You're not bad for feeling as you do. It's life calling you to a new adventure. A new way to be! The old pattern has a place with you and cannot be excluded. It, too, is not bad or wrong. It got you this far. But now it's asking you to resolve its cause and grow.

Typically, a pattern trying to rest expresses through symptoms, and these symptoms butt heads with your heart's desire and point out an imbalance or exclusion in the system that wants to resolve. In the example above, the quiet person starts experiencing symptoms of irritation, frustration, and anger around their self-imposed lack of engagement. The symptom (irritation) is in search of a resolution and will keep on presenting until a shift occurs.

A cursory examination of your life will reveal symptoms—unpleasant recurring emotions, thoughts, and other habits that are trying to get your attention. A constellation can help you to see, feel, embody, and resolve this redundant pattern so you are open and available to create a new one.

Laura was the only surviving sibling of seven children, all of whom had died young. She worked hard to be reasonably happy but was often tired and stressed. She said she felt like "death warmed up." Her presenting symptom was chronic anxiety that she just couldn't shake. And her parents called her a hypochondriac because she was always worried about her health, frequently visiting the doctor to find out what was wrong.

We set up representatives for her mother, father, herself, and her dead siblings so she could see, feel, and explore the pattern of her anxiety. Her representative sat down next to the other siblings and immediately reported feeling the anxiety and other negative emotions that were typical for Laura.

Her biggest fear was predictable: she was afraid that she would die like her siblings. She felt at risk. Like so many other clients with dead siblings or other family members, she had an inner systemic sentence running that said, "My dear siblings, if you couldn't live a full life, how dare I?" As well as producing profound anxiety, that kind of sentence can also drag the living sibling into survivor's guilt. In their hidden loyalty to the ones who didn't live, they find themselves unable to enjoy a full life. Some struggle to complete things (another symptom) just like their siblings couldn't complete a full life cycle. They can start projects perfectly fine, but completing them is scary. It could mean "The End." The opposite can also be true, with living siblings doubling down on everything as if they were living life for all the absent siblings.

Addressing what drove her to go to the doctor, Laura said she had the distinct sense that something was wrong, but she didn't quite know what. She needed an answer so she could relax and know she was going to be alright. "When did you first become aware of that unease?" I asked.

Her face changed and she teared up. "When I was nine, my neck hurt terribly," she said. "It just wouldn't quit. So, my parents took me to the doctor, and he said he couldn't feel anything but that I should have a CT scan just to make sure. My parents took me home, and I never had that scan done."

As we explored the event, she realized that she had wondered if there was something terribly wrong with her that her parents weren't telling her, and that she was going to die like her siblings. She didn't want to worry her mother and father even more, so she kept silent about her fear. Because she hadn't asked the question she needed to ask or been given an answer that could put the anxiety to rest, she came to her own erroneous conclusion that she wasn't okay. The pattern of anxiety and the need to go back to the doctor for answers persisted and became a dominant pattern for her.

When we placed a representative for the doctor in the constellation, immediately Laura's representative went over and stood next to him. Laura burst into tears. "I see it now! I keep going to doctors trying to get an answer from that first doctor about my neck problem and find out if I'm going to be okay!"

That unasked question hadn't been resolved for her nervous system, creating decades of anxiety. Understanding that an unasked question had prevented her nervous system from settling was an eye-opener for her and certainly for me. Her terrible symptoms were gold. They bothered her enough to motivate her to move past hidden loyalties to her siblings (she too should die) and her parents, and to go look for an answer. When she did, the answers were right there in her system.

Amazed at how she'd been living out a systemic family issue, Laura quickly moved from being anxious and exhausted to cautiously facing life with enthusiasm. Recently she shared (with a big smile) that someone close to her had told her she is a regular positive Pollyanna!

Systemic Steppingstone #9:
Patterns Looking to Rest

Patterns that want to rest but can't are pointing toward something in the system that needs to complete or resolve: a question that needs answering, a conversation that needs to be completed, an exclusion that needs to be remedied, a decision that needs to be looked at so balance in the system can occur and the pattern can be resolved.

Write down a pattern that is very limiting for you. Some examples include, "I am hopeless at keeping a relationship," "I'm always short of money," "No matter what I do, I am never good enough for my parents," "I struggle to get paid what I am worth." Speak it out loud. Listen to your words. Notice your feelings and watch your actions, *especially* if they are dogmatic or idiosyncratic. Write down the exact words you use. Can you connect these symptoms to a particular event? It doesn't have to be huge to trigger issues and symptoms.

Once you identify the unresolved, repetitive, or exclusionary limiting pattern, you can finally see what needs to be seen and then complete it. Remember to thank it for being there as a guide and for having gotten you this far.

LEAN IN . . . GENTLY

When I am working with someone, I listen with a lazy ear and watch what's going on with a lazy eye. Bert Hellinger, the founder of systemic work, called this "listening from an empty center." The crux of it is, I watch and listen with pure curiosity and no agenda. I look at body movements and expressions and listen to words, their tone, repetition, emotion, and flavor, because all of that is telling me what lives in a person's system and how. I wait for something to pique my interest enough to want to take a deeper look. Perhaps there is a hint of a pattern. When a client vents or is unhappy, I am intrigued because I know they are on the brink of seeing a pattern that needs to be recognized and resolved so it can stop. Then I follow that prompt and begin asking questions, exploring in 3D, seeing where the symptoms or issues lead and the pattern that wants to stop.

You may be feeling hopeless and trapped. You might tell yourself, "I can't do what I want to do with my life. I do what I have to do to get by. Maybe I'll just take a nap, then I don't have to think about it." When did that start? What was happening for you at the time? Who else in your family might have felt this way? Was anyone else ever trapped or hopeless? Could they not do what they wanted to with their life? What needs to stop?

Listen to yourself with a relaxed ear and eye. Be curious rather than anxious as you go on the hunt for a pattern. Your annoyance, frustration, sadness—whatever it is—is pointing to that existing pattern that wants to be seen so it can stop. It's all a clue. Don't push anything away. Lean into it and understand it. You are literally a living creator of your heaven and hell and a repository of centuries of other people's heavens and hells. All those patterns have happily stomped through generations seeking balance in and for the system, waiting for someone to figure it out and make the leap. They've found their way into your life in the hopes that you will see them and realize that *you* are the change agent.

ASK THE QUESTION

Symptoms of the pattern that's trying to rest or stop are often linked to a prior event in your life or the lives of your ancestors. The pattern is probably filled with dos and don'ts, warnings, and hidden loyalties. After all, that's what's kept it active and alive. However, one simple question really cuts to the chase, revealing the pattern's relevancy. "Is this serving me now?" This isn't the golden bullet, but it is the door opener. If it's not serving, then the next logical systemic question is, "What *would* serve me now?" This question is followed by, "What needs to happen for this to stop or change? What needs to be completed or changed?"

Often what needs to be resolved is a mindset that has resulted from an inaccurate, limiting, or era-specific assessment or interpretation of a certain event, like Laura and her grandmother. I am, quite frankly, stunned and fascinated by humans' inherent need to obey and not ask questions at the cost of their happiness and evolution. I cannot tell you the number of clients I've worked with who tell me that their parents or spouses or bosses were a certain way, and it was "just best to not ask" about what they said or did. Instead, they jumped to inaccurate conclusions and made the other person's words and actions mean that there was something wrong with themselves. Yet with a simple question or two, they realize that they were way off base and have suffered for years for no good reason.

I hear wives telling their husbands, "If you loved me, you would know what I need." Forcing their partner into an assumption—what kind of craziness is that? Or here's another one of my favorites: "You know what you did wrong!" Uh, no, I don't. But based on the look on your face, I may not want to find out!

Assumptions are often unhealthy, but we make them all the time. I worked with Keith, a client who had severe digestive challenges brought on by stress induced by bottling things up. When I asked why he didn't just discuss what was bothering him, he looked at me as though I'd lost my mind and told me, "We don't speak about difficult subjects in our family. It's not polite."

As a child he had been rewarded with his parents' attention when he sucked it up and never asked for something he wanted. His father had grown up wanting to please *his* father, who was stoic and insisted upon the same from his children, admonishing them not to be needy. Any emotion or request was viewed through the "needy" lens, and it became a lovely way to get everyone to toe the line. Deep conversations weren't allowed. Everyone assumed they knew what everyone else was thinking. It was a muddle, and no one was happy. For Keith, his body was making him pay!

Tired of being in pain, he was ready to put down all the excuses and look at what needed to stop or change. "So, what's the worst thing that might happen if you were to speak out?" I asked.

He was floored. He realized that his parents weren't about to disown him and that they would likely get over their disapproval. Keith had been taught that exploring his frustrations was indulgent and bad; now he was learning they actually had purpose and mattered. He realized that there was room for both kindness and manners *and* speaking up and having what he desired. He could see how the old pattern had served him and give it a place in his heart and awareness while also acknowledging that he needed and wanted to do things differently and take his place as a change agent in his family system.

He also realized there were some parts of the old pattern that served him and were worth keeping. His silence had made him really good at active listening. On the flip side, he let go of his learned inability to speak up (a trait he was now seeing in his youngest child) and started asking for what he really wanted. He discovered that there was a *lot* that he'd wanted in life, and this new way of thinking activated a whole different set of neural networks in his brain. He began designing his thoughts, feelings, and actions to fit what he wanted to have and how he wanted to be. As Keith was no longer bottling up his fears, joys, ideas, and desires, or fearing rejection, his stomach and digestive system problems eased within months. At work his associates reported feeling safer around his leadership as a result of his ability to articulate his needs and desires clearly. At home his children were first puzzled and then, as he put it, liberated. They asked so many questions that his head spun, and he had to put the brakes on some of the many wants. But it was clear a door had opened, and an old systemic pattern had been broken.

USING SYSTEMIC WORK WISELY

Systemic work and constellations is like any other transformational approach. You can use it to blame and shame or to flow and grow. The more you learn to speak this language fluently and use it first for yourself, the wiser you become. You are a being in search of evolution. Be wise with the patterns you identify and stop so you can be equally wise with the ones you create.

The first step is understanding that your symptoms are gold and respecting them as part of a pattern that wants to stop and also as part of your system. But learning to spot patterns can be a little trickier than it may seem. Symptoms don't always arrive with clear issues attached. Identifying your real issue and what keeps you stuck is a process. Sometimes what seems to be the obvious issue behind a symptom isn't the issue at all. Sometimes it becomes like peeling an onion—a discovery process that takes you deeper and deeper into your psyche, discovering one answer, only to be led to the next and then the next. In the following chapter, we will explore this layering in more depth as we dive into the explicit and implicit levels of identifying your central issues.

CHAPTER 6

MINING FOR GOLD, PART 1

Identifying Your Issue

Most of us don't see that everything in our lives is speaking directly to us all the time, giving us hints as to what's wrong and how to fix it or what's right and how to amplify it. Maybe a vague uneasiness hits you every morning as you open your eyes. Maybe there is a depression as you finish your work at night. Maybe you experience anxiety or full-on panic attacks. Perhaps there's a relationship that just doesn't leave you feeling good about yourself. However slight or acute your symptoms may be, most people believe that their feelings and the issues they point to can never be resolved. *It's just the way life is.* And then we watch someone else break through and become a star on television or in the news and wish we were them. What did *they* do to be so happy and successful?

Unfortunately, we aren't raised to look to our own lives for cues. Instead, we're given a bunch of social dos and don'ts or religious rules to follow that are supposed to bring us happiness. And when they don't, we think there's something wrong with us. We aren't taught that we are where we are because of a combination of ancestral patterns and personal life events that we have not learned to properly identify and process so we can resolve them, change things as needed, and elevate the journey. We just keep running the same patterns of thoughts and feelings that are driving the same choices and the same actions that recreate the same issues and events down the road. Then we rinse and repeat.

Sound familiar?

If you are consciously feeling stuck, if symptoms keep escalating and you can't pinpoint the cause and you don't know how to deal with them, if you can't find your way out of a repeating pattern or if you find yourself in the middle of a sticky situation that you don't understand, congratulations! Life is pushing you to change. That means you want something different and are open to change. The task at hand is to identify exactly what has you stuck and why it's so persistent and pervasive right now. This is an important step to your transformation.

TIP OF THE ICEBERG

In the previous chapter we looked at how your symptoms are gold. And they are. They get your attention and wake you up to the fact that something is off. Now the tricky part is spotting the real issue at hand.

Sometimes what seems to be the issue morphs into something at a deeper level, revealing that the initial symptom is simply the surface evidence for a deeper systemic imbalance. Simply put, there are layers to your issue. The presenting issue, the *explicit* issue, is just the tip of the iceberg, the surface piece that bugs you, masking the implicit issues, which are the real root of what's happening deep inside you and your system. Keep looking, and you will unearth the *implicit* or root issue that has you stuck. Once you crack that nut and see what's hiding there you can grasp what's really going on, and all the other layers begin to shift in response. In later chapters I will show you how to use your root issue to find your own unique destiny, fulfillment, and success. But right now, finding that implicit issue is the next step.

Here's a great story that will help you get clear on the difference between explicit and implicit issues. Carol came to me wanting to work through something that had happened at work that left her anxious and depressed. Her boss had recently passed away and bequeathed her a lamp. A senior partner had demanded she hand it over even though the lamp had been gifted to her in her boss's will. The senior partner was escalating the situation into a war, telling her the business partners needed it more—that handing it over was "the right thing to do." Carol was locking her office at night so the lamp couldn't be stolen from her and was ready to quit over the demand for the lamp.

Now, a disproportionate response to a situation—Carol quitting her job over a lamp—is interesting. Something more must be going on, right? The explicit issue is the lamp. The implicit issue needed to be uncovered.

As she talked, the tears started flowing, and she clenched her fists. I also noticed that her shoulders were drawn up tight and that she was holding her breath between sentences. Her legs were tightly locked with her feet turned inward, like a child sometimes does. This kind of body response didn't suggest emotion about something happening in the moment; it pointed toward an embodied response to a systemic trigger. So, I asked, "Has something similar ever happened to you before?"

"I always have to give people what's mine," she bit out angrily. "I can't keep doing this."

Aha! We were on the right track. "Can you tell me more?" I prompted.

"I have a habit of giving people my things all the time."

"Why is that?"

"Because it's the right thing to do." She sighed. "I know I shouldn't be so selfish, but can't I just once attend to my own needs?"

Can you hear all the shoulds, musts, and judgments in her words? "Shoulds" tend to be more in lockstep with being loyal to the rules of a system than to our own desire to grow. That one set of rules can keep us stuck tighter than a rusty padlock without a key! I asked why she had to give her stuff away all the time and why it was the right thing to do. To whom was she being loyal? Whose approval was so important here?

"I don't have anything of my own that I love," she blurted out. "I'm always having to give my things to others. Just *once* I'd like to keep what I love!"

Now we were onto something. Look at the words that point out the history, the pattern, and the desire. The last part showed a hint of defiance, a realization that the way things were (when she could figure out what that really was) wasn't working for her.

"Well, it's just a lamp," she continued, her shoulders slumping. "I guess they might need it more."

"So, you think you should hand the lamp over?" I asked.

She nodded. Then she shook her head. "No," she said. "This time I don't want to. I know I should, but I don't want to, and that's the problem. I don't know how to be a good person *and* keep the things I love. I see other people manage it, and I wonder if they're bad and I'm good?"

Notice the back and forth and the judgments. The tug of war between what *she* wants and what something in the system seems to want. I see this push-pull between the personal conscience and the conscience of the system a lot. Of course, the systemic conscience frequently wins out because it's so much bigger and has rules we are accustomed to obeying in order to belong. Hence the stuck-ness for so many of us. How often do you decide you want to do one thing only to follow the consensus of the group? That's the systemic conscience winning out.

"How valuable is the lamp anyway?" I asked.

She shrugged. "It wasn't that expensive, I don't think. But it has plenty of sentimental value for me." Her eyes teared up. "I can't tell you how many hours Frank and I spent working late nights with its light shining on the desk in his office."

She explained that Frank had been a true mentor to her. Although their relationship was strictly platonic and professional, he'd taken her out to expensive dinners a few times, and there had been one or two business trips that had shown her an entirely different world from the limited one she inhabited.

"I really liked and respected him. He was a genuinely nice man. But one thing really bothered me."

"What was that?"

"Well, he had a lot of money. He had a lot of possessions."

"Why did that bother you?" I asked.

"I couldn't figure out how he managed to be such a good person and have so much stuff." She paused, obviously remembering the past. "He did tell me one time that he thought I had a lot of potential. But that I seemed to have a lot of baggage too."

Pay attention to the sentence about being good yet having material things. Carol was revealing just one of so many misconceptions people have about money, keeping them from having a healthy relationship with it. All of this clearly showed that the issue was not about the lamp. All her talk about being good and having nice things, her mentioning "a different world out there" and a boss who "has a lot yet seems nice," clearly showed me we had moved off the lamp and were sitting between two patterns, heading toward the implicit issue.

Just to see what might happen, I set up a constellation containing her mother, her father, herself, and the lamp. The representative for the father moved away and wasn't interested in the lamp at all. The representative for the mother moved closer to the lamp and looked at it with interest, then put her hands behind her back and looked around as though looking for someone else. Carol's representative looked at the lamp and started to move toward it, then stopped and looked at her mother.

"Carol," I said, "do you remember the first time you had to give away something you loved?"

"Yes! I was five, and my mother told me I had to give my favorite doll to another little girl who had no toys. She was living in a shelter with her mother and two sisters. I cried and cried over that doll, and my mother scolded me, saying that giving was more blessed than receiving and that there were so many people in the world who needed things more than I did. She said it was the right thing to do."

That was the moment Carol decided that what was hers wasn't really hers. She made the decision *at age five* to stop loving or even wanting things. In later years, she even refused to have a pet, knowing that she might love it and that it, too, would be taken away from her at any time.

When I asked about her mother and father, she said her mother's family had been very poor. As a child, her mother and siblings would be given Christmas gifts by one branch of the family that they then handed over to their mother to wrap for the other side of the family. They became gift-swap central, never keeping anything for themselves, not even the things they really liked.

At that point, Carol got it. "Of course! We always had to give away our things, even the things we loved, because it was the right thing to do."

That was the implicit issue, the systemic program she'd been raised in, and it wasn't working for her anymore. It gave her constant anxiety. She couldn't hold onto anything, not even money, because someone else needed it more. No wonder she was so angry about the lamp. No wonder she was ready to quit over something so apparently petty.

When Carol started looking, she could see how the pattern of giving things away had begun as a way for her grandmother to save face in the family by having Christmas gifts for others so she wouldn't be seen as a failure. That then morphed through her children into a code of ethics. Carol's mother had carried on the tradition by finding others who needed things, instilling in her children the correctness of giving their things away to those in need. Carol had faithfully repeated the pattern because it brought her praise from her mother and grandmother. She was a saint! But a very sad saint.

She realized that the lamp was simply a repetition of the doll, and that pretending to not want anything was the method she had created to protect her heart. She understood that she really wanted to build a good life and have some nice things that she could cherish and enjoy without feeling guilty about being a bad person.

When I asked her what the scariest part of changing the pattern might be, she quickly replied that she didn't want to give up the idea of being the good girl in her mother and grandmother's eyes. "So, what will happen if this pattern continues?" I asked.

She started to laugh. "I will have a daughter who will hate dolls!"

Carol had reached a pivot point. This time her desire to keep something she loved was stronger than her need to give everything away. The anger she was feeling was a clue that something needed to stop. The senior partner was simply another parent telling her to give up something she loved. Hooray for the senior partner who had pushed her too far!

Which brings me to a very important point. Many times, the apparent perpetrators in our lives are simply the ones who awaken us to the fact that there's an unnamed issue that needs to be untangled and evolved. Start looking around at those who bug you and ask yourself, "Why are they here? What are they triggering?" Chances are they may have something to do with illuminating an issue that needs to shift and resolve for you.

Once Carol's implicit issue was clear, she could clearly articulate what in her current world wasn't working for her. The unmasking process and the truth hurt a little. But it was also a turning point. Seeing the systemic program, she could choose differently and follow her heart's desire. And she started that journey with a simple statement: "The lamp isn't going back! I love it, and it belongs to me."

PAYING ATTENTION

Most times we are stuck because the systemic pattern has more pull on us than the desire to move. So, when symptoms and the issues they point to show up, bless them! It's the higher version of you ringing the bell, calling for attention, indicating it's transformation time.

Moving out of inertia into possibility often shows up as irritation, sadness, anger, and other strong emotions. Be respectful of and attentive to these feelings. When you are angry, upset, and annoyed, *lean in*. You are unconsciously engineering your shift. Sometimes it feels like hitting rock bottom. But hitting rock bottom means you and your body know it's time for something else. It's important to listen to that calling, whichever way it shows up for you. If you stick with it, it will move you past your reasons for staying stuck and take you straight to where and what and who you want to be.

Systemic Steppingstone #10: Finding Your Hidden (Implicit) Issue

When you are feeling stuck or unhappy, ask yourself what you really don't want or like, and then listen. Ask yourself, "What's not working for me right now?" Money, relationships, career, habits? This is your explicit issue. Write it down.

Remind yourself that having an issue doesn't make you wrong, stupid, or unworthy. It makes you aware. It means you've outgrown your current place and you are wanting to make your way to the next level. *Start listening to your issues as prompts to move, not declarations of failure.*

You're like Aladdin at this point. You're about to rub that magical lamp as soon as you can find the darn thing. Well, here it is. Hidden right smack in the middle of your issue.

We've been taught that to moan and groan drags us down to lower levels, and that's true if we're doing it unconsciously or overindulging in the misery and growing the cesspool. But acknowledging suffering as a clue to our implicit issues isn't complaining. It's action.

After you've written down what's not working for you without censoring yourself, ask yourself, "When did I start feeling, thinking, or acting this way? What was happening to or around me at that time? How did I feel, and what decision did I make about what was happening to me in that moment?"

Again, don't censor what shows up. Write down the answers exactly as you say them in your mind. Words and phrases are clues too. We are pretty specific as human beings even if we don't realize it. What dislikes or restrictions have you formed around this issue? Who or what do you judge about that? Whose fault is it?

Once you've answered all that, highlight or circle all the hot words, repetitive words, emotions, themes, and patterns. Write down all the patterns you can see and then ask yourself which pattern is most directly affecting the issue that you have right now. Then see if you can tie it into where you first noticed this happening for you.

When you have that in place, see if this is a recurrent pattern either for you or for someone else in the family. What about it scares you the most? How will your life be if this stays the same? Does this pattern even belong to you? Did it begin with you, or did it happen further back in the system? Do you have unconscious loyalties to the system that are keeping it intact?

The process of exploring an issue is a bit like dropping a stitch in knitting that creates a run all the way down to where it's been dropped. You have to see what's happening in you, then pick the clues back up, row by row, so you wind up with an intact pattern going back to the start. And when you hit on the real problem, boy do you know it! The realization will have you sitting bolt upright in your chair, eyes wide in discomfort.

Once you've hit the spot and the issue with the most feeling, dare to ask yourself one final question: "What would be a really good outcome if this were to change?"

This question begins the pivot.

WHEN IT STARTS WITH YOU

Sometimes we are the ones to initiate a pattern, and *we* are the ones creating the emotional DNA that gets passed down to our children and their children. This may happen in a positive or negative way. Positive emotional DNA is created when we're making decisions and establishing directions that move us beyond the limiting conscience of a system. Sometimes we may feel like we're on shaky ground or even feel like an imposter, but truly, when we expand a system, we are pioneers.

Creating negative emotional DNA happens when an event is so overwhelming that we create limiting thoughts, feelings, and decisions around it. Say you're in a bad car crash. Later you develop a phobia about cars. You can't even get in one. This evolves into a general phobia of traveling and moving about, and you become more and more housebound. This not only obviously affects your success and fulfillment, but can trickle down to your family as your children begin to repeat your patterns.

All in all, transforming patterns—whether they start with us or started far earlier in a family lineage—is up to us. We're in the driver's seat. Yes, emotional triggers can be intense and uncomfortable, and nowadays there's a lot of talk socially about how retriggering may be harmful—that we shouldn't look at what's bothering us and tread warily if we do. However, there is another possibility. *Triggers are helpers.* They are there to offer us insights into what needs to change, and we can use that information in service of our health and movement into lives we love. They are invitations to move beyond fear and distress into creation.

It all begins with you. As an ancient wise one once put it, "Physician, heal thyself." If you can be willing to feel the fear, annoyance, frustration, anger, and impatience for a little while without judging, you will begin to notice the clues that your body and systems are trying to provide that are always in service of you. Then you can move beyond them into understanding. And then . . . transformation time.

CHAPTER 7

MINING FOR GOLD, PART 2

Exploring Your Issue

Before we dive into how to explore your issue, I want to remind you of something incredibly important: the game of life is limitless, and you were not put on this earth to suffer. You are here to experience, learn, grow, enjoy, and love—and then radiate and share all of that.

Your life, no matter what, is remarkable, and there are no constraints on who or what you can become. It doesn't matter if you are a low earner or have been called a "low achiever." It doesn't matter if you're a billionaire who has seemingly done it all. There is no one who can't change and improve their life.

Everything you have done up to now has value. Just like your family system, everything in your life has had a purpose. It all belongs, and it all counts. Everything you chose and experienced or didn't experience brought you to this moment. Don't judge it. Use it. Those who hold onto regrets, struggle. Those who mine for insights and move on grow in wisdom and fulfillment.

Remember: if you show up, you will not only grow up, but so will your children and your community. When you choose to move on, you create a pathway for others. The stronger your sense of purpose and determination, the faster it will pull you past your limiting emotional DNA inheritance and into a whole new realm of possibility.

SACRED WORK

Most people spend their entire lives indulging or dodging their wounds, limitations, and triggers. Uncovering and then exploring personal issues is brave and sacred work that frightens many. But I am here to tell you that *transformation doesn't have to be painful.* The key is realizing that there are gifts in everything that has happened to you. Everything. Once you get this, exploration becomes a joyful process, and the backpack filled with old, burdensome patterns gets lighter and lighter.

Will there be uncomfortable moments? Yes. But they don't have to confine you. Allow all the feelings to emerge. Allow the systemic sentences buried in your subconscious to surface. They will all tell you things. Allow any resistance that shows up to show up. Don't judge it. See where it takes you. Listen to every one of these components. They are breadcrumbs guiding you out of the labyrinth of old patterns that have been keeping you stuck and unhappy. Don't default to judgment and dead-end thoughts like, "Well, I guess I'll never do *that* again! What a jerk I am!" Instead, ask yourself, "Gee, why did I do that, and how can I use that to grow?"

Develop your understanding. Ask yourself the kinds of questions you've been learning to ask. "If I _____ (retreat, fume, fret, withdraw, fight, argue, hate myself, fill in the blank), where will that take me? Who else in my family reacts that way? How has it served them (or not)? Do I want to do something different here?"

If the answer to that last questions is "Yes," then what could you do differently? These are the basic mechanics of exploring your issue and the healthiest attitudes to take into your exploration to make it a rewarding and effective process.

AN EXPLORATION TEMPLATE

Here's another client story that might help serve as a kind of "exploration template" for you to follow. Catherine came to me in her late sixties. After thirteen years of being happily single, she finally decided she wanted to bring a man into her life again. And yet she was plagued with uncertainty. Did she really want a partner? Each of her three marriages had been relatively brief and unsatisfying. Even though all three men had loved her, she was always the one who left. The periods of singledom in between relationships were always longer than the relationships themselves.

"Why am I always dissatisfied with the men I pick?" she asked. "I get into a relationship and end up being bored. And then I leave."

I asked her about her upbringing and family history. "When I was four years old, my mom divorced my dad," she said. "That was in the mid-1950s. I was always puzzled as to why she did it because when I reconnected with my father later in life, I discovered he was a real sweetheart. It never made any sense to me why Mom left him only to marry an abusive alcoholic a few years later. She never left my stepfather, no matter how bad it got. And it got pretty bad."

The need for abuse over love was a multigenerational thread we would pursue. But first we had to discover whether there was an ongoing pattern of leaving men in her family line. "Is it really true that your mother didn't leave her second marriage?" I asked. "And what about your grandmother on your mother's side?"

Catherine thought about it and gasped. "Mom totally withdrew from her second marriage, spending most of her days and nights in bed reading historical novels and drinking bourbon!"

So, Mom left two men who loved her, and drinking alcohol systemically often points to disappearing from a life or a pattern that we can't face. Next we explored her grandmother's marriage. By the time Catherine came along, her grandmother was basically unavailable to everyone in the family, including her husband, because she developed Parkinson's disease in her early forties. "She was like a pillar of salt," Catherine said. "Immobile, silent, and removed."

I pointed out that her grandmother, as well as her mother, had basically left her husband.

"Wow," she said, her eyes big, "I never looked at it that way. I always just saw her as being sick. But she really did leave . . . just in a different way! They both just withdrew!"

In light of this information, I asked her to state the issue she wanted to address, and she came up with the following, more accurate issue: "I always leave the men who love me."

Next it was time to explore the issue in depth by asking a series of systemic questions—which is exactly what you're going to do with *your* issue.

Here are the kinds of questions I asked Catherine to help clarify her issue:

- What are your thoughts about men?

- What are your thoughts about love?

- What are your thoughts about intimate relationships?

- What are your thoughts about leaving relationships?

- Why do you have to leave men?

- Who else left men? (This points to your unconscious loyalty.)

- If you were to not change this pattern, what would likely happen?

- If you were to change this pattern, what might happen?

- What is the outcome that you want from this?

- What one thing do you need to change in your language, thoughts, feelings, and actions to get a different result?

It's not enough to just ask initial questions. Once you get the answers, a whole new crop of questions will arise that will help you explore your issue. I'll give you one example from my list of questions to Catherine.

Her immediate, candid answer to my question, "What are your thoughts about men?" was revealing. "Most men are idiots," she replied. "They're boring and a pain in the ass to have around." She laughed, adding, "Well, I guess that answers why I'm not in a relationship with a man."

Indeed it did.

After she had answered all the questions listed above, it was time to dig deeper. Here are the follow-up questions I presented in response to her statement that "Most men are idiots."

- Who was the original "idiot" for whom all others pay the price?

- If your filter and truth is that most men are idiots, is there even a remote chance that they could appear otherwise?

- How might you give the "original idiot" a place in your heart? What is one good thing that you got from the original idiot? Even if all you can say is "life," be able to identify something good.

- Do you serve your grandmother and mother by repeating their inability to have a lovely man around?

- What kind of man would you really like to have around you?

- What do you need to stop, and what do you need to start?

Catherine had very little family history to go on to answer all these questions. She had no idea about her genetic father's family history, and no family information further back on her mother's side other than a vague recollection that her grandmother's father had been "a mean son-of-a-bitch." Aha! There was more possible harshness from men in her lineage than just her stepfather.

"Was your grandfather abusive?" I asked.

"No," she replied. "He was a doctor and a real caretaker."

"But your stepfather was abusive?"

"Absolutely," she replied. "He never hit either of us, but he was horribly abusive verbally."

If a child comes from an abusive environment, it is commonplace for them to be confused about abuse and love. A social systemic sentence around the world is, "Parents love their children." So, when a parent is abusive, the child comes to associate abuse with love.

"Did your mother ever tell you why she left your real father?" I asked.

"She did say something really weird one day. She said, 'He loved me too much, and it made me feel guilty.'"

In other words, both Catherine's loving father and her loving grandfather went against the pattern of abuse that may have started with her great-grandfather. Although there was no way to find out, it was possible that Catherine's grandmother had felt the same way about *her* husband, the kind and caretaking doctor she had left by getting sick, because she had experienced abuse from her own father and now her husband was acting contrary to the original emotional DNA that had been laid down confusing abuse and love.

Catherine's mother stayed loyal to *her* mother by leaving the kind man who loved her and marrying an alcoholic abuser. Catherine broke the unconscious loyalty by *not* marrying an abuser. But loving relationships with kind men were dull after being around the constant drama of her own mother's pain-oriented relationship.

So, who was the original idiot for whom all others pay the price? Was it her great-grandfather? Somebody before him? Her grandfather? Her stepfather?

"I don't know about anybody else, but my stepfather sure fit the bill. He was judgmental to the point of ridiculousness and always had to be right, even when it was painfully obvious he was wrong. I remember thinking as a little kid, 'Doesn't he know he's setting a terrible example for me? When is this idiot going to grow up?'"

"Is there any possible way you can hold men as being something other than idiots?" I asked.

As she contemplated that question, she realized she really didn't think all men were that way at all. "I've known a lot of wonderful men in my life, including my husbands, who were smart, affectionate, decent men."

"Is there a way for your stepfather to have a place in your heart? Is there something good that he did?"

"Well, he insisted that I be raised on a farm," she said, smiling. "He had it in his head that the only place to raise a child was in the country, so I have him to thank for thirteen incredible years spent living out in nature, riding horses, and having a ball. Being raised on that farm was my salvation and set the tone for the rest of my life."

Score one for the idiot.

Consciously admitting that most men she had known were smart and loving enabled Catherine to see that her knee-jerk assessment of all men as idiots—her original assessment of her stepfather—was a strong pull to a deep systemic trance based on a pattern created in the past and not at all true in the present. Understanding that she had emulated her mother's pattern of leaving men simply because there was no "spice" in the relationship, she was able to open up to the possibility of having an intimate relationship and set about imagining what kind of man would interest her and keep her engaged. She became acutely aware that she could have spice and nice without abuse.

See how using systemic questions to explore your issue works? When Catherine came to me with her issue, "Why am I always dissatisfied with the men I pick?" the obvious starting point for questions was about men and relationships and her thoughts on those subjects. The line of questioning developed naturally from there in response to what showed up.

If you're working on an issue by yourself, be as present and thoughtful as you can when developing your questions, and then be as candid as you can in your answers. It helps to record rather than write your answers because we tend to be more spontaneous and truthful when speaking than when we write. Then listen to your replies and ask questions about them. Drill down. You'll know when you've struck gold.

LOOK FOR THE GIFTS

Another thing to do while exploring your issue is to be sure to look for the gifts in your journey. For Catherine, it was hard to imagine there was a gift to be found in having been raised in an abusive family situation fraught with alcoholism and violence. She wondered why she couldn't have been brought up in her real father's home—a home that felt so much kinder and more welcoming. With some deep reflective exploration, she realized that, although it had been painful, growing up with an "idiot" at the family helm had provided the impetus for her to become incredibly self-reflective, self-reliant, rational, and capable. She realized that had she been raised in her father's home she would likely have been a whole lot more complacent and perhaps not had anywhere near the number of incredible life adventures (starting on the farm) that she'd had.

And the gifts didn't stop there.

Her mother's chosen lot in life, trapped at home with an abuser, had ignited in Catherine a determination to get out in the world, pursue a television career, travel, and live a happy, joyful life . . . with a husband or without one. Finally understanding the systemic roots of her original issue, "Why am I always dissatisfied with the men I pick?" she developed a new set of systemic sentences to live by.

"Look, Mom! Look, Grandma and Grandpa! See what I can do? I can find answers! I can be happy and embrace the goodness and beauty life offers! I can take my full place and uplift my life and the lives of others to make this world a better place, and I can have a relationship that is kind and spicy. Men are lovely and welcome!"

What a turnaround.

DIY CONSTELLATIONS

Systemic questions are the first step in your exploration of your issue. But there are times when I am working with a client where we may not get the full sense of what is going on until we set up a constellation and step into the 3D version of the issue.

The same thing may happen for you. If you are reading this book and doing this work at home and you feel stuck or as if you have hit a wall using systemic questions, I would suggest you set up a constellation using whatever is at hand as tokens to represent the different parts of the issue you are exploring, like you did in Systemic Steppingstone #4.

The point of creating a constellation is to dimensionalize and bring your issue to life and engage multiple senses so you can see, touch, stand in, hear, and sense what is happening. Placing the representative tokens on the floor in a room is helpful. You want to experience a *felt sense of the situation* so your body, brain, and mind can process and rewire your new thoughts, feelings, and actions. Remember, mind and body are *not* separate. When your body experiences a constellation, it gives your mind a new frame of reference. A new view of things can instantly change your entire mindset and thus your reality.

The trouble with trying to work issues out in our heads the way we are accustomed to doing is that we can't perceive things like direction, connections, distance, engagement, and relationships between each part of the system. We also can't view the system from multiple vantage points. All these dimensional pieces give insights and invite questions and mindful reassessment of our thoughts, feelings, and actions about the originating event that created our issue.

A constellation creates embodied experiences that take you where you want to go. And there is no one who can't do this. I didn't do a constellation with Catherine because the foundations for her issue were clear just from systemic questioning. But if we had done so, here are the different kinds of constellations I might have suggested she set up. Again, this is to give you an example of what you can do at home to clarify your own issue.

Catherine's issue: Why am I always dissatisfied with the men I pick?

Desired outcome: An intimate relationship I am happy with.

What we're looking for: To whom does this pattern of dissatisfaction belong, where did it start, and how do I change it?

1. Set up a constellation of all the men in your life. Be sure to include a representative for yourself. Look for patterns and relationships.

2. Set up a constellation with you, your family, and all the men in your life. Look at the relationships not only between men and women but also between women and women and men and men in the multigenerational pattern that has you stuck.

3. If there's enough information, set up a constellation of your mother and all the men in *her* life.

Once you've set up the constellation, look for relationships. Who is close to whom, and who is farther away? Just that initial picture in front of you begins to bring insight to what may be happening and illuminate your issue. Links, relationships, and patterns begin to emerge along with those pesky little jailers, our unconscious loyalties.

I have women who tell me men don't stick around in relationships only to find that a man in their family system left, or was lost. The original woman who was left may have said something like: "You can't depend on a man, they all disappear." Then generations of women are loyal to that saying and, in effect, to that first woman who lost her man. There seems to be an inner systemic sentence that goes something like this: "Dear Mom. If you couldn't keep a man, I won't either." And now all the women unconsciously align with the governing sentence in the family system.

It's important to note that men don't have a chance in such a system.

And if you think you don't have any unconscious loyalties, just ask yourself why you like tea without sugar or a particular kind of candy, why you vote a certain way or think some things are wonderful while others are unacceptable.

As you recognize your unconscious patterns and loyalties, a couple of things can happen. First, you can choose to keep repeating the now conscious loyalty because the alternative is too uncomfortable for you. In which case the next generation gets to deal with it, and you get to stay where you are. Or, if you consciously explore your issue, the door to insight, possibility, shift, and transformation opens.

Systemic Steppingstone #11:
A DIY Constellation

If you have limited space for a constellation, use something like chess pieces or sticky notes on a tabletop—any setup that gives you a sense of space and orientation. If you have more space, consider using pieces of computer paper on the floor. With Systemic Steppingstone #4, you took a first look at a constellation. This constellation is going to add layers of direction and tie your issue to a principle. If you can figure out which principle your issue is tied to, that is an indicator of what's needed to resolve the issue and create balance in the system. "I don't belong" can turn into "Now I belong." "I give too much" can become "I receive gratefully." "I always have to take care of everyone" into "I can allow myself to be taken care of too."

Write down each character and component in your constellation on a separate piece of paper with an arrow at the top to establish direction. Don't overthink it. Set up your issue dimensionally on the chess board or with papers on the floor in the way that feels right for you. (A quick note here: I ask you not to overthink it on purpose. Your first layout often most closely reflects the reality of the situation for you. Go with that and watch it unfold.)

Remember, all you are doing right now is exploring your issue. You are looking for the unconscious loyalties (and their owners) that keep your thoughts, feelings, and actions stuck. You are also looking for patterns. *This is not yet about resolving what you see*. For now, you are simply being fully present and identifying and awakening insights.

To find your way into what's happening, identify which of the three principles of belonging, order, and balance of give and receive is involved (chapter 1). Add more characters as needed.

Before you start moving anything around, stand back and take a look. Take a picture, or at the very least, draw a diagram. You want to note this first layout and be able to compare it with your final one so you can see the movement that happened.

Focus on your issue. If you are using a chessboard, feel each piece as you move it. If you are using a whole room, allow yourself to move between the pieces as needed and pay attention to what you feel.

Write down what you say, think, and feel about what you're experiencing. Once you have those systemic sentences, patterns, and dynamics in mind, see if you can find where they originated and with whom you are aligned. If you are prompted to move any of the characters, keep doing so until they come to a stop. At each step, notice your thoughts, feelings, actions, and insights.

Stand in or near the space of any one of the characters you want to explore and see what it feels like to stand in their shoes. Keep watching and observing. As you explore any of the limiting or unconscious loyalties, ask yourself what this has cost you, and pay close attention to your body's and your brain's responses. Ask yourself, "To whom am I loyal in the ways that I _____ (suffer, stress, play small, or whatever applies here)?"

On your journey to the center of you, you are going to pass through many generations. In the process you will encounter what has held you back, discover the gold that's been there all along, and uncover your pathway to the amazing being you really are. Doing this work has the power to profoundly change your world and then the world around you. Unlock your chains and manifest your power.

CHAPTER 8

THE PIVOT

Transforming Your Issue

As I have mentioned before, the top priority for a system is to survive. But its highest ideal is to thrive and grow. A lot of constellation work stops at the resolution of an issue. The pattern is complete. The event is over. You go home and let the old pattern rest while letting all the new information work its way into your psyche and spirit. Yet many clients would ask me, upon completing a constellation, "Now what?" I started exploring, and I realized, "Wait a minute. We are creators! We don't want to stop at 'issue complete.' What's the rest of the story?" I realized that the completion of one pattern is the beginning of a new pattern. Without the one completing, there's no place to start, and without the new one emerging, there's no place to go. Thus, the pivot between the two patterns, old and new, emerged.

When you pivot, it means you are moving *from* something *to* something else. You are changing direction, level, and perspective. In systemic terms, you are saying "Thank you" to your roots and "Hello and welcome" to your wings.

In the beginning, the "from" is your guide—what you don't want anymore or your point of departure. That leads to the "to"—what you deeply desire. You have to get clear about what you want. It doesn't have to be monumental, and you don't have to know the full endgame. But the goal has to be something clear and attainable; otherwise, it becomes a nebulous, unquantifiable head game. More fun, more "me time," more money, more independence, more creativity, all of the above—start in that direction. But you also have to give yourself a place to land in the form of creative, measurable goals: "I want to go to the beach twice a year. I want to have $10,000 in savings. I want a healthy, happy relationship."

In chapter 4, I talked about how transformation seems magical. You see a pattern and wow! Everything shifts, and life is never the same again. However, transformation is also a process of persistence, commitment, and conscious work. Yes, insights happen in an instant, and they can be game changers. But you're the one who has to run with the insights, apply them to your life, and transform your emotional DNA by teaching yourself to choose differently, think differently, talk differently, act differently, one choice, one thought, one feeling, one statement, one action at a time.

BLOCKS TO PIVOTING

Sometimes we are deeply, *unconsciously* wedded to our issues despite our protests to the contrary. We are stuck in the systemic story line, feeling the feelings and thinking the thought patterns of other generations. Seduced by the systemic trance, we can end up doing what we know is bad for us, but it feels so hypnotically familiar (and thus so "right") that we succumb anyway. We want to escape the prison, but to go forward, we actually have to move in the direction of the solution. It's not about escaping from something. It's about heading toward what we want and standing in *that* systemic energy so strongly that it pulls us out of the limiting systemic belief.

One of the subtlest blocks to progress is still being at the stage of *wanting to want it*. You say you want to change, that you want something new with all your heart. But then you don't do anything to make it happen. When this occurs, it might just be a matter of timing or, more likely, an unresolved loyalty to what has you stuck. Your heart, your head, and your body aren't in a state of cohesion. You want to want what you want, but you aren't passionate enough about what's beyond "stuck" to do anything to achieve it. Often in this state, people tell me, "I just want to get out of my stuck place." So much energy still resides in the old pattern that they can't yet invest in creating the new.

The systemic way out of this is first to realize what you're doing, and then to choose one new thought and let it in. Then feel one new feeling. Experience it fully and give it a place, and then look at one new action to do. And then do it! Again, it doesn't have to be a big thing. Think about that book you've always wanted to write (or any other dream that is a heart's desire or a strong pull). I mean *really* think about it. How would it *feel* to have that book out of your heart and onto paper? Would that perhaps be you realizing a dream? How does *that* feel? With that adventure in mind, choose to get up fifteen minutes earlier five days a week to deliberately move toward completing that book that's been brewing in your brain. Momentum is a Newtonian force in this world, and it works as well with personal actions as it does with a boulder rolling downhill. The momentum gained by thinking one new thought, choosing it, and investing in it, by adding one new emotion and expanding it, and then taking that one tiny action ignites the sense of "can do" and moves you past your past. You start gathering steam as you go along, and then one day, you find you're in a whole new place.

Another block to change is believing you have to have every step and all your goals mapped out before you even start. Don't do that. You will defeat yourself before you even take the first step. Transformation is a wonderfully elevating process. Take it one step at a time and notice and celebrate the steps that you take no matter how small they seem. Sometimes you have to just sit for a while, embracing the truth that you want something different for yourself and that something different is possible. Whether you sit with this new truth for five minutes or five months before you start to build the excitement and emotions that fuel your path all the way to completion, it doesn't matter. Just realizing there is another possibility is a huge systemic shift.

Take Catherine from the previous chapter. Her knee-jerk assessments about men and intimate relationships had been in place for decades. If she thought her shift had to happen overnight and leaped onto Tinder or Silver Singles and started developing a romantic online profile with marriage as an end goal, she might have been paralyzed with fear. Bear in mind that a shift in perspective can happen in an instant, but the unlayering and rewiring that follows can take time. Instead of thinking she had to instantly do something with her newfound insights, she allowed a sense of wonder and a growing appreciation for men to slowly kindle, activating new neuronal networks and laying down new neural and systemic pathways. No longer in defense mode, she gradually became more available to the other sex and the idea of a possible relationship as she created and welcomed new ideas about men. And, within a matter of weeks of her first session, a very intelligent doctor friend asked her out to dinner!

So, all you perfectionists and heavy-duty planners out there, ease up. Give yourself a break. Breathe. Remember, the first shift is just the opening. Let it in and let it flourish.

Another way people can block themselves from transformation is by elevating the value of suffering and struggle. Socially we have quite a few systemic sentences supporting both. "No pain, no gain." (Thank you, Jane Fonda.) "Success is born of struggle." Or how about "To live is to suffer." (Thank you, Friedrich Nietzsche.) Sometimes we can see an issue and its impacts clearly, yet we stubbornly cling to whatever it is that is hurting us out of a deep subconscious belief that we deserve to suffer, or that suffering is valuable, or that we shouldn't let others suffer alone. Or we forget all the suffering we've already done that got us here.

Here's a quick story of what I'm talking about. Christina wanted to succeed in her acting career but didn't think she deserved a leading role. She suffered from paralyzing guilt that she'd carried since she was a young woman and was chosen to play the lead in a local theater production. Her chief competitor for the role died a few months later. No one had known that the girl was ill, but Christina carried the burden of not having stepped back and given the girl the part she so desperately wanted before she died.

After that, Christina would rock every part she played in every theater company she worked for, but she would never take the lead. Even though she could see that the girl's death hadn't been her fault and her suffering and guilt were doing her no good, she couldn't let it go. When we set up a constellation using representatives for Christina, the girl, and guilt, nothing happened. It was obvious that something else was in play, so I added representatives for her mother and father. Immediately, the representative for guilt moved closer to Christina's mother.

"Why is guilt so attached to your mother?" I asked.

Christina burst into tears. She was an only child, yet her mother had been extremely emotionally distant. One day Christina overheard her mother say to her father, "I don't deserve the blessings of a child!" When she questioned her father, he told her that her mother had been driving when an intoxicated teenager ran out into the road in front of her car and was killed. Even though her mother was exonerated, she had shut down completely and never spoken about the accident again. It was as though she died with the girl who was killed.

"I do remember that she was awfully fond of saying, 'An eye for an eye, and a tooth for a tooth,'" Christina said.

I pointed out to Christina that sometimes when we cannot easily connect to a parent, we may find a way to bond with them covertly—which is what Christina had done by connecting to her mother through a life lost and the guilt that came afterward. Her mother wasn't willing to give up her guilt, and the question became, whether Christina would be able to do what her mother couldn't. Or was the blind love and a tie to an unreachable mother too much for her to give up?

It didn't help that, socially speaking, guilt is an acceptable emotion and is sometimes even viewed as praiseworthy. The solution here was to give the girl who'd died a place in the family system—and find a way for her death to be remembered thoughtfully. That allowed the guilt to subside in favor of its elevated counterpart—purpose.

Another block to pivoting is guilt over not being good enough or worthy enough to move ahead. These kinds of blocks show up in thoughts and statements such as: "I'm not worthy enough. I'm afraid I might leave people I love behind. I might make others feel bad about themselves if I get ahead." Or "I might find out I'm as bad as I think I am!"

An unconscious addiction to pain, guilt, and suffering is a way to belong to a larger global system that accepts suffering as inevitable and even admirable. Think Christianity, Judaism, certain traditions in Buddhism, women in general, being Black or Hispanic or Native American, and, these days, white men too. Living in any of these systems, it's easy to believe that transforming may cost you membership in your tribe.

The way to move beyond this kind of mindset is to wrap your head around the fact that if you rise up, you will not lose the system you came from. Rather, you will *expand* the system you've been trapped in, and you'll do so joyfully. When you do that, *everyone* in the system can systemically shift their own patterns and mindsets upward. If you can't do it for yourself, make the shift for others.

Reluctance to move forward is also often tied to the fear that something awful might happen. "I might fail. I might get hurt! If I take responsibility, it's all on me!" If "voices" like that show up, it helps to imagine the worst possible outcome and then see if that has already happened to someone in the system. Who else in the family took responsibility and had a bad outcome, and how does that resonate for you? After identifying the root event, it becomes a matter of building a strong case for moving forward rather than staying put.

One last block I'd like to mention is the one that says you need permission to change or move forward. Often I find that we get to a point in a constellation where the client is about to pivot, and they stop and look at me or a representative as though they are asking for permission to move. The questions to consider here are: Whose permission do I need to move or change? Who will I upset or disappoint if I do (or don't) change? Why is this movement causing me to hesitate? What is my biggest fear if I do (or don't) make this move?

If it's a strong enough loyalty to someone or something, you will hear yourself come up with all sorts of excuses: "You know what? I am fine where I am." Or "It's not that important." Or "I just can't do it today. I'm too tired, sad, mad, busy. Maybe one day." Be aware that your pull to the unconscious loyalty is stronger than your need to move toward something else. Either your current situation isn't causing you sufficient pain to motivate you to change (the proverbial stick), or you haven't built a strong enough case or purpose (the carrot) to move you past the hidden patterns and unconscious loyalties.

Bottom line, transformation is magical, but it isn't magic. It is inspiration and motivation married to patience and persistence. It's about being willing to look and then act. And if it takes you fifty or a hundred or a thousand times looking at your systemic patterns, then look. If it takes a thousand questions, then ask them. Be willing! And don't ever be afraid to dream! Pain is a powerful motivator to change. But passionately happy dreams and desires will take you a lot further and give you a much grander destination. Don't be afraid to dream, and dream big. Don't be afraid to go for and enjoy the carrots.

TAKE YOUR FOOT OFF THE BRAKE

The minute you identify what wants to stop and what wants to start, your brain and whole-body system begin rewiring. It's not possible to be the same anymore. You can create obstacles and blocks and delay the process. But sooner or later—through you or another person in your system—change will occur. We've talked about blocks. But what about the people who make the shift from issue to goal happen easily? What are they doing differently?

They have taken their foot off the brake. They have run out of reasons to delay, or they are so passionate about where they want to be and what they want to experience that they are all in. They *know* what they want. These people ask questions with clarity devoid of excuses. They allow their thoughts to flow and *feel* their way wholeheartedly into how it will be. They feed the day-dream, and they often have a clear goal. They love where they are going, and they don't listen to discouragement. Even when the past and the systemic voices whisper to them (or yell at them), they keep moving forward. If they need to look back, it's to search for wisdom and insights to help navigate their new path. They continually say "Yes!" to their dream and anything that takes them closer to experiencing it. They move from anxious and doubting to clear, determined, and engaged. They acknowledge their "buts" without getting trapped in them, and they start asking, "What do I need to do differently?"

You have probably heard motivational speakers and spiritual teachers talk about "letting go," but they don't specify *what* you should let go of, which leaves some people confused. So, let me demystify letting go. It means you put down all the excuses and limiting points of view and conditions that show up in order to let something entirely different come about. I do this in two ways. I ask myself if the way it is right now is working. If it's not, I write down my excuses and points of view, read them, and give myself permission to think, feel, and act differently. *Relationships can work, rich people aren't greedy, I am smart enough to figure this out.* Then I remind myself that the new answer wants me to find it, and I make an agreement with myself to park the old ways of thinking, feeling, and doing for a week. You let all the old stuff go. And that's when things start to shift. When I'm changing, so does my world.

Transformation doesn't have to be hard. One step at a time will get you there. The good news is, if you are reading this book, you already have a sense that a bigger life and a greater you are waiting. All you have to do is make the switch and learn to pivot.

THE PIVOT

A pivot is the central point of change—the turning point. The first rule of the pivot is this: don't let anyone define your goals, purpose, or path for you. Your goals, purpose, and path are yours to choose. If you want to start small, that's fine. If you want to go big in a hurry, that's fine too. It's your life, your dream, your choice, and your journey. If you want other people's opinions, fine. But in the final analysis, always, always listen to your heart, your gut, and your brain, and don't let anyone put you off track.

Secondly, moving from where you are to where you want to be means you can no longer be a victim. The minute you see your issue clearly and you choose something different, you move into the role of creator. You move into your power by discovering what you want, saying "yes" to it, declaring it, and moving toward it. That doesn't mean you're not allowed to have moments of doubt, temporary uncertainty, or moments of feeling defeated. Those feelings are a part of anyone's journey. It's just that you can no longer play victim and let those old multigenerational feelings stop you anymore.

Might this be a little scary? Absolutely. Is it possible to just let it all go and move forward swiftly with apparent ease? Absolutely. Take Hannah for instance.

She came into the constellation event angry and loudly vocal. She criticized everything that she heard and complained about every exercise she was asked to do. She kept using words like, "Not on my watch" and "I have a voice, and I will use it." You could hear her coming down the hallway after breaks as she cornered some new person and told them what she'd observed about them. Continually disruptive and abrasive, when her turn to work came, she almost left. Finally, she agreed to stay and do her constellation, *if* she could work it with her back to the rest of the participants.

Her issue? Hannah felt she hadn't had a place with her family since she was a child. Her family despised her and wouldn't let her in. Everyone was quiet and polite yet aloof. She felt guilty and cursed and was at the workshop because she was desperate to connect with her four siblings and mother and find a way to belong. "Mother is constantly saying, 'Manners maketh the man and ladies are quiet,'" she said. "She's always telling me I'd do so much better if I were a little quieter!"

But being quiet was something Hannah not only could not do; it was something she was vehemently opposed to. "If someone has something to say, it's absolutely, undeniably necessary that they do so," she declared. Not surprisingly, she confessed that people found her to be too much, perpetuating the cycle of isolation outside of the family circle, stopping her from belonging anywhere.

Her language caught my attention because it was right in line with the rest of her behavior. I asked about being quiet, and she told me that her mother and her aunts and uncles never spoke out when it counted. It was well known that her uncle had not spoken out when he found out someone was defrauding the family business, and it almost ruined them.

This made some sense of her insistence on using her voice, but it didn't explain her loud, demanding, abrasive nature. We set up representatives for Hannah, her parents, her siblings, her uncle, and the family business. The representative for the family business lay down on the floor, and her uncles and aunts went and stood next to him, eventually sitting down next to him. After a while, her father's representative lay down on the floor and almost immediately her mother's representative sat down next to him. Hannah's sibling representatives all grouped around her. At that point, Hannah's representative reported wanting to be sick and leave the room.

Hannah went pale and quiet and couldn't speak for a while. "The damn voice!" she finally bit out. "It always comes back to the damn voice! And the damn manners!" I asked her what she meant. And this was the story that unfolded.

Hannah was five and her father's little princess. Life was great until he got sick. One afternoon she was sitting in the living room with him while the rest of the family was across the road with one of the aunts. Suddenly Hannah's father clutched his chest and fell to the floor. Terrified, she ran across the road to her aunt's house for help. As she ran into the living room, about to shout, "Daddy needs help!" her mother put her finger to her lips—the family sign for minding your manners and being quiet. It took fifteen minutes for her mother to finally allow her to speak.

Her father was dead when the family got there. After the funeral, her mother went into her bedroom and didn't emerge for a month. The siblings asked Hannah continually why she hadn't spoken out. After that, nobody spoke about it again. As her mother and siblings grieved together, Hannah knew it was her fault and shut herself out.

As an adult, Hannah was clear that silence was no longer an option. Manners and silence had caused her father's death, and she raged against manners and pretty much everything and everybody. And yet silence and manners were required in the family, so she couldn't belong—doubly so since it was her fault her father had died. She had no idea how to process her father's death and the circumstances, so she boomed and yelled and disagreed and interrupted all the time. The system kept trying to speak through her, and she had no idea what it was saying. She only knew that she didn't belong and that she had to speak. Something had to stop, and something else was wanting to start.

Years after her father's death, the coroner told her older brother that her father had died instantly and that nobody could have done anything to save him. Her brother stayed silent about that until Hannah was much older, by which time the thought patterns of guilt and exclusion had been set. In her mind she was guilty, cursed, and didn't belong.

I placed a representative for the coroner next to her brother and asked them to tell Hannah it wasn't her fault. Hannah began to sob as she listened and really heard the facts as if for the first time. Her representative sat down next to her mother and father, and then, after a while, she stood up again and shook her head. Hannah nodded and explained that she had consciously decided she couldn't just dissolve into silent grieving like her mother and siblings, even though the situation had been so heavy.

As we looked at the picture in front of us, she realized that her siblings were so busy looking at Mom, who was looking at Dad, that they couldn't see her. They had all locked into that pattern. It wasn't that Hannah was bad; it was that they were lost in grief and focusing on Mom. Hannah was stunned. Her lifelong conclusions were unraveling in front her. Now that the coroner had spoken, her guilt no longer had a home either.

"I have been sad and guilty for so long over nothing," she said as she realized her exclusion wasn't what she had thought it was. I asked what might have happened if she'd joined her mother and siblings in their deep, ongoing grief and silence, and that stopped her in her tracks.

"I think I would have died too," she said. "Instead, I was free to choose something else, and I did. I thought they didn't want me, so I was angry, and I struck out on my own. It gave me a life."

Notice how Hannah's conclusions are starting to change here? As we watched the constellation unfolding in front of us, I asked what a good outcome might look like, and her eyes widened. "I don't want to be afraid to look at the truth anymore," she said. "I don't want to be afraid to show people what happened or who I am."

I asked if we could swing the constellation around so she could continue it in front of everyone, and she nodded. We shifted the constellation back into the circle and continued. She was at the pivot point, yet she was still focused on what she *didn't want*, so I asked again. "What would a good outcome be? What do you want?"

"I want to stop shouting at my family," she said, and she stopped. "I never got to say goodbye to my father. I need to move on. I want to speak out when it counts but not all the time. It's exhausting." The tears flowed.

We walked over to her father, and she told him how much she missed him and that she wished she could have saved him but realized that she couldn't. She said goodbye, and her father's representative stepped back. Then he offered a simple sentence: "Use your voice wisely, it's how you belong."

"What was your father like, Hannah?" I asked.

She wiped away her tears and sniffed. "Dad? He was loud, proud, and he didn't give a damn." The whole room laughed, and so did Hannah.

"I am my father's daughter," she said, making the room laugh again, and then she got serious. "I *am* my father's daughter," she repeated, and she started to shake. "I am the one who loves life just like he did. He had a big voice, and he told me when I was little that the truth would set me free. I thought he was crazy, and yet here it is!"

She looked over at the representatives for the rest of her family and told them: "I belong just like Dad did."

Her representative moved closer to the family group.

I asked about her career, and she started to laugh even as she was crying. "I'm a public speaker!" she said. "My niche is speaking up for those who have no voice. I am a spokeswoman for several large public causes, and I am known for calling out hidden truths and deliberate silences as I see them."

The entire room erupted.

She laughed again. "I didn't realize that the biggest lies were the ones I was telling myself. I have never not belonged. The silence in my family gave me a purpose. Now I can use it differently." She was quiet for a moment, then added, "It's so strange, I've been wanting to shift for a while."

See how Hannah is coaching herself forward? Recognizing and speaking and assimilating the new truths she was seeing?

At that point, Hannah put her hand over her heart and stood deep in thought for a bit. Her father's and mother's representatives moved behind her and placed their hands on her back, and that made her stand up straight. She lifted her head, grinned, and said, "I want to teach people to use their own voices. I want to teach others to speak out when it's necessary with eloquence . . . and manners!"

Her declaration was clear. Not long after that constellation, Hannah began to teach a series called Next Door Strategies, eventually becoming a much beloved coach, speaker, and mentor to top executives.

A CLASSIC PIVOT

As angry and jarring and initially reluctant to engage as she was, Hannah came in with an agenda to shift. Even though she couldn't face the group at first, she still wanted to work. She admitted in the beginning to feeling a cross between excitement and nervousness. Her emotions wanted to shift into elevated emotions, and she was intrigued by a sense of new possibility. That got her into the constellation, at which point she lowered her defenses and committed to the process. She moved out of her headspace and old patterns and allowed herself to see what was in front of her with fresh eyes. She didn't balk or refuse to look. Throughout the constellation, she stayed engaged and invested in allowing for a completion and a shift.

When I do a constellation, I look for a physical, visceral shift in a client, which Hannah exhibited as new insights unfolded. She later reported that she could feel her body relaxing and releasing old patterns that had kept her tight and angry. At that point, her body became her friend, working with her brain to rewire old, limiting patterns even as the constellation was progressing.

As the new insights unfolded, she let them in, naming them and owning them. Right there she was rewiring her thoughts and feelings, activating new neural networks, telling herself new truths, and reaching new, nurturing conclusions. She committed to belonging and saw the importance of using a softer, more elevated set of emotions. She embraced her new vision of herself and her new purpose in life and, after the constellation work, immediately set about applying her new knowledge in her life and work.

If she could do it, so can you!

Systemic Steppingstone #12: Transforming Your Issue

You know what your issue is. Write it down on a piece of paper and put the paper at one end of a room on the floor. (If you only have a small space to do this, use a sticky note on a table.) Now, look at your wants or heart's desires. Write them down on a new piece of paper and place it at the opposite end of the room where you can move around it.

Notice what you think and how you feel around those dreams and wants. Do you feel different over here as opposed to standing next to your issue? Can you name the new feeling? Can you allow for its possibility without censoring or negating it? Try it on like a new outfit. *Feel* your way into this. Part of the pivot is being open to something different, so allow for that new possibility to emerge into your current world.

With the two pieces of paper at opposite ends of the room, go back and stand on the pattern trying to rest— the place you are at now in your life. Then look across at the pattern trying to emerge. Slowly move toward the pattern trying to emerge. Listen to your thoughts. Feel the feelings that stir in you. Notice where they are in your body. Notice your actions and reactions. Do you move across swiftly? Do you stop? Reverse? Hesitate?

If a sentence pops up, write it down and place it in front of you. Does it become a limiter or an enabler of movement? If you find yourself reversing or moving sideways, explore that. Is there something you need to complete? Only move forward once your thoughts and feelings say "Yes." Remember, your body is a helpful compass as you accomplish this, and your brain is supplying the thought-clues you need to know what's going on inside you.

As you are moving forward, notice if you need a resource or support. Did you just have the thought that Uncle Jimmy would be a great person to help you promote the business you're dreaming about and walking toward? Write his name down and put it on the floor where you're standing. See if it makes a difference. If it helps, hold onto it. If it doesn't, place it to one side. It may be needed later, or it may contain an old thought that needs to be resolved. Keep moving and adding resources and ideas as they come up, adjusting language, thoughts, and actions as you move.

If you find yourself feeling overwhelmed, it's okay to take a step or two back until you settle down again. This is not failure. You took a step. Notice what is stopping you and where that sits in your body, and complete that. Once you are able to move, take the next step. Have patience and be kind to yourself. It pays off. In fact, that may well be a new step for you. "Be patient and kind to myself." Write it down and put it on the floor next to you.

You may have to tell yourself a new thought, practice, or feeling a number of times. Great! How many times have you told yourself how bad or unworthy you are until you believed it and made it your truth? Once you get to your goal, feel it. If it doesn't light you up, it may be too small or incomplete. Rest for a while, then retest it.

See if anything needs adjustment. Don't worry if something doesn't feel right at first. Just adjust, like Goldilocks, until everything feels just right. Once you have those new thoughts and feelings, ask yourself, "What is one new action I can take that makes this even more of a reality?" *And take that step.* The new step may in turn lead to another new thought and then another new feeling. Now you are not only resolving issues, you are also building dreams.

PART III

DIGGING DEEPER

Into the Heart of the Hidden Language That Runs Your Life

CHAPTER 9

DISENTANGLING SENTENCES OF DOOM

Sentences of Resolution

You think you just open your mouth and talk. The bigger truth is that you give voice to your system, though most of the time you don't notice it. Passed along from the mouths of our ancestors, words slip happily out of newer mouths, wondering if the brain will alter them enough to transform our perceived limitations into wisdom and illumination. Your language is *key* to cracking the wonder of you.

The words we speak and think not only shape our daily interactions, they also shape our lives. Words mold our reality on an individual and also global level, creating war and peace, castes and creeds, hope and despair, joy and sorrow. An entire system of thought and action can be dismantled in one short sentence: The war is over. Your disease is gone. You have the right to vote. One word—"guilty"—can end a life.

Everyday heroes and people who excel intentionally use words to create the thoughts, feelings, and actions that support what they want to be and do. They make a habit of using positive words of self-affirmation. "You are bold, you are brilliant, and you are beautiful," says plus-size model Ashley Graham to herself. "There are no mistakes, only opportunities," says actress Tina Fey. "I am the greatest," said world champion boxer Muhammad Ali. "You can have anything you want, if you want it badly enough," said Abraham Lincoln.

Examine the way unhappy, unsuccessful people talk, and you hear words and sentences of doom over and over again. "I knew I couldn't do it. Everything I touch turns to ___. There's just no winning. I'm always the slow one. I'm too stupid to understand." Instead of lighting a fire of inspiration that sets them free, they constantly feed the flames that make them burn with shame, anger, and guilt, condemning themselves to living lives that are deeply unsatisfying. And sentences of doom aren't just typical self-derogatory examples like these. *Any systemic sentence that drags you down and keeps you stuck is a sentence of doom because it dooms you to more of the same.*

"Patience is a virtue" until it isn't. "No pain, no gain" is the perfect setup for a life of continued suffering. "Asking for help is a sign of weakness" destines us to a lonely life of struggle and effort. The good news is that words and sentences of doom can also serve as our liberators because they contain the seeds for identifying and stopping limiting patterns in their tracks once we see and acknowledge them.

But until we see and face a limiting systemic sentence straight on, like an alcoholic standing up for the first time at an AA meeting and declaring, "I'm an addict," a sentence of doom is a not-so-silent saboteur. Seeing it and acknowledging its existence are unbelievably powerful. Just as admitting "I'm an addict" isn't a declaration of failure, admitting to a systemic sentence of doom is a declaration of *what is*. It identifies the truth of what's going on and calls it by name, allowing investigation into how it has been created and how it can be disentangled and transcended.

GHOSTBUSTING

Once you accurately voice and acknowledge the sentences of doom that have plagued you for so long, the things you've been telling yourself on a loop can no longer continue to stealthily create the truth that defines you. The pattern has been seen and acknowledged. It has been "ghostbusted."

Kevin is a perfect example. Every day he told himself he must work hard. And every day he came home so tired that he needed a half-hour nap just to be with his family in the evening. His sentence of doom? "A real man works until he drops to give his family a good life." It was a line he learned from both his father and grandfather, who both worked until they were in their eighties. They seldom took a day's vacation, and both dropped dead from heart attacks.

His grandfather had lost everything in the Great Depression but rebuilt a decent life for the family through sheer slog. His father fared a little better but was always terrified they would lose it all. Kevin's family, on the other hand, had a great life. He had positioned their life so he could retire if he wanted, but his sentence of doom was condemning him to repeat his father and grandfather's fate. Kevin's anxiety was high, and his doctor warned him that the stress and overwork were going to kill him.

"I'm afraid we may lose everything! I have to be prepared!" Kevin said as his fists clenched and sweat broke out on his forehead. The acknowledgment was clear. This was his issue.

"So, what's the actual truth of your situation?" I asked him.

"My financial advisors tell me we have enough for me to retire and live the good life until I'm about one hundred and ten," he admitted. Just saying that out loud, Kevin started laughing. Then he broke down in tears as he realized he had been speaking his father's and grandfather's words, and that they didn't belong in his mouth. "A real man works until he drops" was a sentence that had ignited his work ethic and produced real wealth, and for that, he said, he was truly thankful. But that was the past. The words were no longer true.

Often the words and sentences we hold in our minds, locking our bodies into certain emotions, are specters that rattle around like ghosts going bump in the night, holding us in fear as hostages to the past. When put into proper context and spoken aloud, they don't sound quite as logical as we think—or even make sense.

"Can you tell me how you feel about your current circumstances and all the hard work you're doing?"

"I'm exhausted," he said. "All the men in my family were exhausted." He exhaled heavily, closed his eyes, and his shoulders drooped. For a moment I thought he was going to fall asleep. Then he opened his eyes and said, "This is killing me too."

Aha! Another, even more powerful acknowledgment of what the reality was *outside* his systemic trance. Then, all on his own, he came to what is called his sentences of resolution.

"I can't do it anymore. I am not going to work until I drop, too. My family has a good life. We are safe." As he said the words, he shook his head as if in disbelief at the current truth that had finally been spoken. With those words, he laid the patterns of fear and slog to rest. The sentence of doom that had been a solution for his grandfather and father was finally set down as no longer necessary to Kevin's life.

SENTENCES OF RESOLUTION

As we have just seen, a sentence of resolution is an accurate, insightful, and finalizing sentence often used during a constellation after the acknowledgment of the pattern, giving it the command to "Stop!" It is part of the pivoting process and creates a sense of completion that releases the brain and body from a long-held pattern or position. It's typically accompanied by insights, such as Kevin's when he said, "We are safe."

Sentences of resolution are declarations such as:

- I'm not doing this anymore.

- I won't leave like they all did.

- I'm putting this burden of responsibility down. It's too much for me.

- I won't suffer like they did anymore.

- The struggle has to stop now.

- Doing this over and over again is getting me nowhere. I'm ending this.

- I'm done with the drama!

- I can't continue being unhappy.

- I won't enable their _____ (sadness, addiction, fear, anger, abuse) anymore.

- I will no longer keep spending like there's no tomorrow.

The above sentences of resolution are examples of a pattern ending, possibly a multigenerational or multi-event one. When you are exploring your issue and you hit a bottom-line insight like Kevin did ("This is killing me"), the sentence of resolution often comes effortlessly and usually reflects the hidden pattern ("Real men work till they drop. I'm afraid we will lose everything"). In Kevin's case, his sentences of resolution clearly evolved from his sentence of doom ("I can't do it anymore. I am not going to work until I drop, too").

There are frequently tears or an exhale when you arrive at the statement of resolution, and you have a clear sense that something is finally done. Stating an accurate sentence of resolution brings a feeling of release. You can breathe! Often we don't even know a negative pattern has had us in its grip until we pay attention and notice our less-than-positive self-talk. When we finally hear ourselves and the terrible things we've been saying, thinking, and feeling about ourselves, others, and the world around us, we get to see the direction our words have been taking us and wake up. We see the pattern, wake up to the unconscious prison, and make acknowledging statements, and then declarations of resolution rise up through us like a total energy wave. We have no need to search for the words. They are already there, waiting to be released.

So, what do I mean by *accurate* sentences of resolution? Everybody has a unique language. It's idiosyncratic in the ways it belongs to only you and your system. Kevin's language was about working "until you drop." Different words, phrases, ideas, and feelings will speak to your heart, mind, and gut as they may have done for generations. When you use the right language to identify your pattern and sentences of doom, you may experience relief, peace, exhilaration, or other emotions. You may exhale loudly or yawn. I often hear participants say, "That feels right." They express deep emotion or a sense of completion and peace. There is no doubt. Your heart, head, and gut all get it, and you are now in a state of clarity about what lives in you that you don't want to perpetuate anymore.

When you come out with your sentence of resolution, you want to be sure to complete the pattern that is trying to rest using words that your brain and body can accept or buy into at a deep level, words that tell you, "This is done," paving the way for strength and direction to emerge.

HALF LANGUAGE

Before we get into the sentences themselves, I want to point out that most of us are born and raised using only half of our language—the half of unhappiness, fear, poverty, grief, despondency, hopelessness, and limitation. Starting early on, many if not most of us are told all sorts of negative things—that we're stupid and unattractive, that we lack grace and appropriateness, charm and wittiness. We are negatively compared to others and taught to believe that we are substandard in every way. We're told, "You'll never amount to anything," or "You're a fool, just like your father."

We're taught that we are sinful creatures and that we're not supposed to think of ourselves and be "selfish." We don't run with sticks because we're told we'll fall and poke our eyes out. We're not curious because curiosity killed the cat. We're taught to eat our food out of guilt because other children in the world are starving. We're trained to be proper and do for others, to go along with the status quo, to follow the rules, and not to make waves.

Rarely do we hear the other half of our human language. Whether it's English, French, German, Spanish, or Chinese, how often are we encouraged to think of ourselves with positive words? How often do we hear, "You can do anything you set your mind to!" or "Things always work out for the best." How often are we told, "You're amazing!" Brilliant? Beautiful? Smart? Courageous? Delightful? How often are we told that human beings are kind, loving, generous, and thoughtful?

And when we are complimented, when we are told good things about ourselves, what do we do? We demur. We brush the positive words aside. We shrug and say, "It was nothing," or "You're too kind." In other words, we don't let the positive half of our language in the door. It catches us off guard and unbalances our negative perception of ourselves. We hear the words, but we really don't—can't—believe them. But the bad stuff? The negative comments? The racial slurs? The catty, nasty things we hear about ourselves? We take them instantly to heart. And if these barbs come from our parents and other loved ones, the stake is driven all that much deeper into our hearts.

Bottom line, if we're not getting the powerful "other half" of our language from others, out of necessity we must get it from ourselves. And getting it is a *must* for your transformation.

HERO OR ZERO

Take a moment to notice whether you "hero" or "zero" yourself when it counts. Do you typically beat yourself up or elevate yourself? In new or difficult situations, do you naturally go to hope and excitement or fear, unhappiness, and self-doubt? Do you withdraw or engage? How do you feel when you hero yourself? How do you feel when you zero yourself?

Humans tend toward at least a small amount of catastrophic thinking because the human brain is wired to pay more attention to negative experiences than positive ones. In psychological parlance, this is called a negativity bias. The reason we're wired this way is because the brain is constantly on alert for danger. It's purely a survival instinct—a habit we perpetuate until we wake up. Repeated enough, limiting, negatively biased thoughts and feelings can generate patterns that create an uncomfortable, limited truth that is then passed on as though it were an ultimate truth in the system. From this "truth" come multigenerational sentences of doom that commonly lead to unreasonable personal expectations that can make our lives miserable.

I remember one client who came to me to address general anxiety. The systemic sentences she'd learned from her perfectionistic German grandfather, who was a surgeon, and then her mother, who was a nurse, were, "If you're going to do something, do it right," and "Only compare yourself to the best." As medical practitioners, "getting it right" was literally a matter of life and death. The original sentences were helpful and important. But my client wasn't a medical professional. Nevertheless, driven by these systemic sentences, she treated every situation in her life as if it were a matter of life and death, obsessing about being perfect. Over time, these family sentences had wormed their way into her psyche to the point where she was always challenging herself to be the best at everything—academics, sports, business, lovemaking, cooking—you name it. She was relentless about pushing herself.

Once she saw what she was thinking and how those thoughts were driving her, her general anxiety eased. But her real breakthrough came a few months later as she consciously *applied* the new way of thinking. She had taken a temporary position as an office assistant before making a long-distance move across country. She had never done office work before, was not a professional typist, and was only mildly familiar with the computer system she was instructed to use. All the same, by the end of the first week she was browbeating herself about how slowly she was doing the data entry work she'd been assigned. And then she caught herself.

"I was sitting at the desk, beating myself up," she said, "and I suddenly went, 'Wait a minute. I know what this is about!'" She immediately launched into more affirmative self-talk, acknowledging the issue and the real truth. "This is my old perfection pattern. Doing a good job is important to me, and I'm doing it right. But I've never done this kind of work before, and so I'm a little slow. Big deal!" Then she used one of her sentences of resolution: "I refuse to compare myself to others anymore." From that point on she got off her own back and all was well.

Systemic Steppingstone #13:
The Empowerment Walk

There are three parts to a systemic pivot, which I will pull together in the next section, but let's begin here. As you pivot from the pattern that wants to stop to the pattern that's trying to emerge through you, invite yourself to make today the day you are present with what's really happening so you can move into and through it. Use this exercise to mark the day your life changes for the better as you step into your journey as a creator.

To gain a felt sense of this important part of the pivot, take yourself outside for a walk or find a space where you can talk to yourself out loud. And I mean LOUD.

Think about your issue, situation, or condition—the thing that really bugs or limits you—and start talking it out. In your own words, describe the fundamental fear or limitation. Don't try to be eloquent or edit your language. Express what lives inside and what you're feeling using the exact words that you typically use. Here are some examples:

- I'm always on the losing side.

- I never get it right.

- I feel utterly worthless, powerless, or hopeless.

- I feel like I'm always the scapegoat.

- I'm always scared and anxious.

- Everybody but me is getting ahead.

These are all acknowledging statements of the perceived truth of what's going on for you. Pay attention to the way you're acknowledging the situation. Ask yourself:

- Am I making myself the hero or zero here?

- Am I making someone else the hero or zero?

- Do others in the family, business, or organizational system share this way of thinking?

- Is this something that only I do, say, or think over and over again?

- When did this start for me? What situation or event initiated this issue?

- Is there a specific trigger that reignites this issue?

- Is there a time of the day, week, month, or year when this happens?

- Where else do the words I use to describe this issue or situation creep into my vocabulary?

- How does this limit or upset me? How much is it seeping into my everyday life?

Remember to speak all this out loud. Keep walking and talking until you run out of things to say. It doesn't matter if you have to say what you have to say a dozen times in a dozen different ways. Just let it all emerge. Your body will know when you hit those "right on" words and emotions. And you will know when you are done.

Now stop for a moment. Find a place to sit down and lean against a tree or plant your feet in the sand. Whatever works for you. Just be present and ask your tired, angry, sad, frustrated, or frightened self what you want to say about thinking, feeling, or doing what you've just acknowledged. How do you really feel about it right now? How do you *want* to feel about it? Let's use the above acknowledging statements and create some statements of resolution from them.

Acknowledging Statements	Statements of Resolution
I'm always on the losing side.	I can create my own wins.
I never get it right.	I'm capable and make wise choices.
I feel utterly worthless.	I have a lot to offer, and I am excited to share it.
I'm always the scapegoat.	I am no longer carrying other people's burdens.
I'm always scared and anxious.	I am safe and can take care of myself.
I'm sick of feeling hopeless, sad, or powerless all the time.	It's time for me to recognize all the good that I have and all the good that I am and focus on building that library.

Other common sentences of resolution can be statements like:

- This has cost me too much. It's time to invest in my own growth.

- I need to do this differently.

- It's okay for me to start feeling _____ (happy, hopeful, excited).

Keep repeating your sentence of resolution. Repeat it until you *feel* its truth or change it until it fits. You'll know because you will feel it. Note: I cannot overstate the importance of feeling what you tell yourself. You do it with the negative stuff; now it's time to do it with the good stuff. Let it sink in deeply. Notice if your mind is wandering, trying to steer you off topic. Your sentences of doom are out there, and maybe you are really listening to them for the first time and seeing the insides of your prison walls. Sometimes we wander off target because the view is too much!

You will have hit pay dirt when your body starts to react to what you're saying. Notice what's happening in your body. What are you feeling? Emotions? Sensations? Where are they in your body? Your body's reactions can be gentle and fleeting or powerful and jarring. Accept it all as it comes as you *feel* your sentences of resolution.

If you need to cry, then cry. If you feel like you need to lie down, do it. If you want to rock, yell, laugh, dance, shake your fist at the sky, throw something, do it! Don't censor the prompt, *follow it*. Sometimes there is a systemic movement that needs to be completed for the pattern to stop. I have seen people cry and not be able to stop because they were crying for generations who *couldn't* cry. If your body makes a movement, follow it, and listen to it. It is speaking to you in the only way it knows how. If you're not feeling anything, that's okay too. Blankness or resistance is an indicator that you are hovering right at the edge of the goal.

For some, this may be a very quiet process without big emotions or body movements. The point is to stay present and be aware of the words or phrases that stir you in some way. You, the magician, have summoned your self-constructed or multigenerational demons into the light and are looking them in the eye so that now they, and you, can rest.

If at any point this process feels overwhelming, please stop, and know that you have taken some steps and that it may just take a few more powerful walks or sessions like this to unwind fully. Remind yourself that *this is not self-indulgent!* (Who has sentences of doom around not expressing "too much emotion" or "getting melodramatic"? Raise your hand!) No. This is you finally getting to express what needs to be seen and heard. It is the beginning of change for you and part of the pivot to healing and transformation.

When you can acknowledge your issue and name your sentence(s) of resolution from your deepest place, without any excuses or justifications, you are finally ready to lay down your self-constructed prison. When you can look even the most awful situation or pattern in the face, it is yours to change. This is you moving out of blindness into wisdom.

Once again, state your acknowledging sentences clearly and firmly, recognizing how this has lived in you. Then, once again tell this pattern or mindset clearly, using words that stir you, that IT IS DONE.

Once everything has calmed down, go back and state the pattern, acknowledge its place in your system, and then declare your intention to let it rest. Listen carefully as you speak. Feel any residual reactions in your body. Now . . . rest. Don't be alarmed if your legs shake a little or your heart is beating faster. I'm sure David's legs shook after he slew Goliath!

Congratulations! This profound moment of awakening is a moment to remember! Place your hand over your heart. Take a deep breath in and thank your heart for being present as you teach it how to feel a different feeling. Then touch your fingers to your temples and thank your brain for its ability to think one new thought. Settle your hands over your gut and thank it for switching from survival into sensing your highest good. Finally, make sure you say "Thank you" to the issue or pattern that has now gone to rest. It created solutions for those who came before you and took you on a path of adventure leading all the way to this moment where something new could emerge.

Mark this time on your life-event calendar and in your heart, mind, and gut. Add a note to your journal that says something like, "Today, I chose a new life. From today on, I am (strong, happy, healthy). The words I speak, the feelings I feel, and the actions I take all reflect this new me. This is my new truth." Whenever I do this alone, I look around for something to symbolize what has happened. There is always an object that will stand out a little. Maybe a stone, a flower, a penny, something that is speaking to what I have just uncovered and laid to rest. I take it with me and place it somewhere I can contemplate it for a few days or weeks and listen to what it is trying to say to me. I know it's there for a reason. Everything has a purpose.

So, look around you right now and find something that speaks to you. Don't overthink it or try to analyze it. Just trust that it is there for your growth and advancement. Maybe it's a picture you need to capture. Allow that to speak to you and the pattern that you are laying to rest for the next while. Whatever it is, let it become a reminder of the great work you have done today.

CHAPTER 10

PORTALS OF POSSIBILITY

Sentences of Re-Solution

Now we come to the final part of the pivot, the "what's possible" side of language. The first part was about gaining clarity on your issue, the pattern trying to rest, and the pattern trying to emerge. The next part of the pivot was acknowledging your issue and developing your sentence(s) of resolution, creating a statement of finality that brings a limiting pattern to a close in ways you can feel and that bring a sense of relief, excitement, and completion. The third part of the pivot arises out of building firm sentences of "re-solution" on top of our sentences of resolution.

Sentences of *resolution* complete an old pattern. Now there is place for a new solution, or what I call a re-solution. What worked before may not work now, so we move beyond resolution to re-solution: the new solution.

Sentences of *re-solution* are part of your mechanism for conscious growth, for changing your current direction. They reflect a change in your thoughts, feelings, and desires, activating new neural pathways, setting the stage for new decisions and actions that reflect the new you. They are the galvanizing agent for building what will come next in your life, providing inspiration and opening up new pathways to explore who you *really* are—who you're capable of being and becoming.

Possibilities have always been part of our lives, but most of us haven't been given the vocabulary of affirmation and creation that will enable us to actualize them. Sentences of re-solution rely on elevated thoughts, feelings, and emotions for possibility, inspiration, motivation, staying power, and direction. They light up the mind, body, and spirit, tapping into the other half of our language and the other half of our soul—the slumbering giant—demonstrating loudly and profoundly that there is something more available to us than the ordinary life we are leading right now.

BUILDING ON SENTENCES OF RESOLUTION

Sentences of re-solution have the flavor of sentences of resolution, which contain all the coded language from your past and previous generations—language that means something highly specific to only you. Including these words in your sentences of re-solution is especially important for full blossoming to occur. Here's an example of what I'm talking about.

I had a client called Harry whose parents were both deaf-mutes. All his young life, he had to interpret for them. He didn't like that his parents were different, and he hated being the different kid at school. He felt underprivileged and limited by his background, and yet he developed a successful career as a motivational coach by taking himself on as his first client. When things were dire, he imagined how good life would be one day. He created sentences of resolution, like, "I can't carry my parents' burden anymore," and "I have to speak out."

As his career blossomed, he developed a compelling need to become a top motivational speaker. He did well but couldn't get the top gigs. His stumbling block as a speaker was his inability to start off strong. He would fumble through the first minute of every speech, then pick up steam, wowing his audiences by the end. When he came to me for help, I pointed out that spoken language was not his first language. His first language was American Sign Language. If he could reframe the old embarrassment around being the "different one," and *include* his past and all his language capabilities, he could find his truest voice.

Building on his sentences of resolution, he developed powerful sentences of re-solution such as, "Being different makes me unique," and "Using all of my languages gives me an advantage."

No longer rejecting a part of himself, Harry decided to start all his speeches using sign language. Today Harry is a top motivational speaker, just as he dreamed. He recently flew his parents in to see him speak at a big event. Do you see the full circle right there? Harry did fine with sentences of resolution. But building on his life experience, creating sentences of re-solution, transformed him and took him to the heights of success.

CREATING SENTENCES OF RE-SOLUTION

Here are a few examples of acknowledging statements, followed by sentences of resolution and then re-solution:

Acknowledgment	Sentence of Resolution	Sentence of Re-Solution
I am afraid of being seen.	My invisibility comes at too much of a cost.	My being visible brings gifts to the world.
I feel lost.	I have my place in the world.	Taking my full place, I can see new possibilities and act on them.
I don't belong.	I always have a place where I belong.	My sense of belonging inspires me to include others.
I feel empty. Always giving to others is exhausting.	It's okay for me to receive too.	I am a master of receiving joyfully and abundantly.

Systemic Steppingstone #14:
Creating Your Sentences of Re-Solution

So, how do you find your sentences of re-solution? Here we go!

Step one: Generate the climate for conscious change. Allot yourself some uninterrupted time, and find a space where you can relax and think and not be disturbed. If possible, find an inspirational place to sit or walk. Play a piece of inspirational music if you want. Switch your phone off and remind yourself why you are doing this. You are creating transformation!

Step two: Take some deep breaths and acknowledge the family system of which you are a part. Everyone and everything that came before this moment has contributed to this opportunity. Imagine your ancestors at your back, their hands pushing you forward into the future. Tell them you are moving forward and ask for their blessing. Even if you don't know your family system, you will feel the connection if you allow it. Breathe in their blessings and breathe out their burdens. If your family system was dysfunctional or even cruel, if you can't imagine anyone giving you anything but grief, bless the fact that they have made you who you are today: a determined being set on creating change and a marvelous new life far beyond anything they could imagine. (Frankly, if you're coming from an abusive or dysfunctional background, you're somewhat lucky. Most people in your shoes are more focused and determined than others to change.)

Step three: Give yourself permission to go as high as you can today and imagine what you really want. You have acknowledged the old pattern. You have given it a place and set it down, and you have found the power of resolution. Now, allow yourself to dream of where re-solution can take you . . . to the things you want to do, create, and have, the experiences you can revel in that will take you higher and inspire you to create even more.

Don't censor or judge. Just imagine and feel happier feelings. Visualize what you want, as much as you want. You'll know when you've hit something important— something that brings a "Yes!" to your heart, brain, and gut. You'll feel a sense of excitement. Your body will feel lighter. Your heart will open. (For me, my "Yes!" always arrives with a fist pump!)

Maybe it's only the briefest flicker of a feeling. That's okay. Zero in on it. Don't let it get away. This is where the gold lies.

If your mind kicks in and starts saying things like, "Yeah sure. That'll never happen. Who do you think you are?" realize that's the old pattern speaking, not the new one. You know all the old words and emotions attached to that voice—the pain and depression, the hurt, and the loneliness. Remind yourself firmly, "This is the voice of the past and the pattern I am setting down." Return to your imaginings. Return to the elevated feelings they evoke.

"Yes, nice. But what if it doesn't happen?" whines the old pattern.

Well, most of the scary stuff we conjure up doesn't happen either. But that doesn't stop us from thinking all sorts of negative things. Remind yourself that you really have nothing to lose and everything to gain and that the only person keeping you at less is *you*.

Step four: Now that you've imagined all sorts of cool, wonderful possibilities and felt the good, high-vibration emotions, choose what makes you feel the best. This is what you're going to focus on as you create your sentence(s) of re-solution.

Holding onto those good feelings and armed with a deep breath, speak your *sentence of resolution*: "I can't do _____ anymore." Or "_____ isn't mine to carry." Or "I don't want to be sad like _____ anymore." Whatever your sentence of resolution is, speak it now.

Step five: Look for the gift from that sentence and see how you can use it to form the antidote sentences: the sentences of re-solution, the new direction. Here's a simple example. I once had a participant who cried a lot. In fact, once she started, she couldn't stop. The women in her family line had abusive husbands and bore their abuse stoically. They expressed no emotions. They just got on with their awful lives at the mercy of men who weren't kind.

My client realized she was weeping the tears of all the women who couldn't express their emotions. But she was tired of feeling sad and crying all the time. I asked if she was unhappily married, and she said quite the contrary. Her husband was a wonderful husband and father. She had broken the old patterns of abuse and stoicism, but not the pattern of sadness. When I asked her if she had any grandchildren, she lit up. They were her pride and joy. I asked her what she would like to teach them, and she started to smile.

"I want to teach them to laugh so hard that they cry tears of joy," she said. "They have a wonderful grandfather. If I can teach them about joy and good men, that would make me happy and keep them safe too."

Her acknowledging statement was, "I cry and feel sad all the time." Her sentence of resolution was, "I can't bear the burden of these sad tears anymore."

Her sentence of re-solution? "Watch me be the role model for joy and gratitude. Let any tears be tears of joy!"

To discover your sentences of re-solution or antidote sentences, try out different sentences and notice where you feel them in your body. When you speak the right, resonant words, you will experience a sense of relief or excitement or happiness or some other positive emotion. Try the words on. Don't edit yourself. When you're in love with your sentences of re-solution, you're in the right spot.

Step six: Once you have the words, speak them! Many people report feeling like they are standing on holy ground when they find the words that invoke their deepest desires and dreams. And that's exactly right. *Your sentences of re-solution are the language of your soul.* You want to make these sentences your new normal so you can fully experience the adventures that belong only to you.

Step seven: Take a break and relax. Positive emotions and positive sentences of re-solution are brand new muscles, and you've just done about a hundred emotional push-ups with these babies. Don't rush to get back to work or some other task. It can wait. Take the time to soak in the vibrations of what you've just created. Bask in the warmth of those words. If you feel like it, take a shower or lie down and rest a little.

Step eight: Feed your new creation. You don't hatch a baby chick and say, "My job is done." You have to feed that little baby or it dies. Remember all the old neural networks in your brain? The firing patterns of the old thoughts are still there. And they've had years to entrench themselves. Be kind to yourself if you find yourself slipping into old patterns of thought. But don't stay there. Keep exercising this new set of muscles. Keep repeating your sentences of re-solution. Write them down and put them in places where you see them all the time. Take imagination breaks and re-envision your dream . . . the place you're heading toward, the new you that you are becoming. Add any new, empowering sentences and feel any good new feelings that arise.

Step nine: Don't share your new path with rainy-day folks. Nurture it quietly until it's ready to make its public debut. And don't keep checking to see if it's okay. You know what you're doing. You are feeding your dream good words and higher vibration emotions.

Step ten: When it feels right, set up a small step or goal you can reach just to show yourself that this is really happening. When you reach it, make sure you acknowledge it. Celebrate your wins! Take the time to be thankful and appreciate what you've done. Then take the next step, and then the next.

The more you build on your sentences of re-solution and the feelings they evoke, the more the excitement grows until this newer version of yourself becomes the reality. The results are becoming evident in your outer world. You are a victim no more. Your destiny is upon you. You are the captain of your ship. And you know it.

AND THEN . . .

Occasionally ask yourself: "So, what do I *really, really, really* want?" No limits, no reality checks. Just, "What's the most incredible thing I possibly can do, be, or have?"

For me, a formerly poor, unemployed immigrant from South Africa, one of the most far-out, incredible things I could imagine was having a time-share at my favorite place on earth, Disney World. I knew what the goal was,

I was clear—but the obstacles! "Only rich people belong there." "I have no idea how to get that kind of money." "I'm not good enough or nearly magical enough to belong there." "It's an unrealistic dream." All the old language. I acknowledged it fully. Then one day, instead of coming from a space of emptiness, my resolve and determination and pure excitement kicked in. *I wanted that timeshare!* No excuses. I kept quiet so no one could discourage me and feed me my old language. I moved to watching my limiting language and replacing it with, "I can belong here too. I am figuring out ways to make this a reality. I am plenty magical enough to belong here." I allowed myself to see myself walking into that timeshare and sharing it with the ones I loved, and that meant that every spare cent I received knew where to flow. I had given it a place to grow that was larger than my limits. It was growing into my dream. I reminded myself that if I could do it once, then I would know I could build out my dreams in so many areas. I just needed to co-create one dream with the universe to show myself that I could do it everywhere in my life.

The first time my family and I used the timeshare, it was literally a dream come true. Instead of watching others walk in there, condo keys in hand, I was the one unlocking the door. It was a stretch for me at the time. But getting there gave me such an incredible feeling, I was eager for more and bigger creations to come.

Reaching for ever-larger dreams is how we evolve. So, every once in a while, stretch your dream muscles even further and know you have the ability to fulfill those dreams!

CHAPTER 11

THE BIG GUNS THAT RUN THE SHOW

Meta Patterns

B y now you understand how you inherit patterns of thoughts, feelings, and actions from your family system. That they cascade down through the generations, waiting for you to give them your own flavor and twist, hopefully strengthening and positively evolving them before you pass the patterns down to the next generation.

But where did these inherited patterns come from originally? Why did our ancestors make the choices they did? What drove them to those choices? One answer lies in meta patterns arising from meta events that set into motion vast patterns of thoughts, feelings, and ways of operating. Meta patterns affect large numbers of people, coloring perceptions and choices, unconsciously creating both stifling limitations and incredible possibilities.

Meta patterns are the big guns—gender, religion, war, famine, pandemics, diasporas, natural disasters, politics—that run the world and influence nations, whole peoples, and cultures. They have large effects and create powerful patterns and emotional DNA. Epigenetically, these patterns affect subsequent generations, creating mindsets that are the broad, sweeping shapers of whole societies that in turn affect smaller groups, trickling on down into family systems and individuals.

Each meta pattern adds a layer of hypnotic "sleep," which we often experience as a sense of inevitability, fate, or just "the way things are" here on planet Earth. This, of course, is what we call a systemic trance. However, like family systems, meta patterns also offer us the opportunity to grow and evolve . . . once we see them.

Each of the following meta patterns could easily be a book in itself, and I'm not going to get into great detail. My purpose in this chapter is to simply bring these patterns to your attention so you can review your own system in their light. We cannot learn from that which we do not see.

GENERATIONAL JUDGMENT

Evolution is a step-by-step process. What worked for one generation likely won't work for the next precisely because we are evolving. Unfortunately, we tend to demonize what came before us, judging our predecessors for their beliefs, lifestyles, and actions. Even as the survivors of World War II were sitting around watching John Wayne movies, reminiscing about the liberation of Europe and American soldiers' heroism, their children were marching in the streets shouting anti-Vietnam War counterculture slogans like, "Make love, not war!"

We also judge our successors. We look at the "youngsters" who come after us and call them reckless and irresponsible precisely because we are not seeing the world through *their* generational lens, facing *their* generational issues. We sneer at the future, unable to see beyond the limits of our old rules. Instead of celebrating the steps forward and the steps behind us, each generation excludes the other instead of learning from each other.

We can sometimes fail to put into evolutionary context what looks to us now like errors and limitations. Those were the solutions the system came up with for its time and place. When we only negatively label our forefathers and mothers, we exclude their lived wisdom from the system and set the stage for old patterns to repeat.

Growth comes with a commitment to look at and learn from past and future generations with appreciation and informed perspective, not with hate, blame, and judgment. Instead of labeling things as wrong, it is so much more helpful when we notice that life happens in steps—that we are all standing on "our step," looking to take the next step up. When old and new systems collaborate, we benefit broadly. If we can garner wisdom from the past and be open to and curious about the future, we take our foot off the brake and grow and elevate. Realizing that the conscious creation of positive meta systems and patterns of cooperation is what shifts us all toward greater possibilities, the great sleep of humanity fades.

GENDER AND SEXISM

Sexism, which lives largely in our language and actions, has a long history. As a meta pattern, it has been and will likely continue to be pervasive for a long time because sex occupies much of our lives. Our gender roles are evolving rapidly, yet if we don't see that we're evolving and acknowledge our growth, we will be troubled by this evolution. We'll remain fixated on the individual misconduct and inflammatory issues raging in the daily headlines and lose the big picture, blaming this person and that group instead of finding ways to come together to support mutual growth.

Male-female gender issues comprise an enormous meta pattern based in mistrust, judgment, and exclusion. Sexist prejudice is also aimed at the LGBTQIA+ population. Each gender and each sexual orientation is equally part of patterns of judgment, exclusion, and disrespect, yet other genders and sexual orientations are often still viewed as aberrant. Bottom line, we judge the "other" instead of valuing and embracing each other and asking what we can learn.

Overall, people yearn for the freedom to express who they really are instead of being stuck in rigid gender roles. Many women develop careers out in the world and find satisfaction and fulfillment with that as their primary focus. There are many women who want to be homemakers and stay-at-home moms. There are men who want careers and other men who prefer a domestic lifestyle. Family structures are being reshaped. Being a working woman used to be shameful; now it's pretty much a given. Being a stay-at-home dad used to mean there was something wrong with the man; now it's a choice. Notice that women and men have always had these choices, but the meta patterns of socially acceptable gender roles have been so sweeping and rigid that, up until now, we thought we were not allowed to venture outside those tight boundaries.

Of course, some changes have only recently become possible. Physically changing genders was not an option until 1917, but modern medicine has now given people the choice—*if* they can internally shift the still existent meta pattern (belief system) of "there are only two genders in this world, and you're stuck with the one you're born with."

Meta patterns tend to shift slowly. Despite the tremendous strides we've been making, when I set up constellations, I still see women who feel unworthy and diminished, demanding equality yet feeling undeserving thanks to their emotional DNA. I see multigenerational anger toward men, and judgment, resentment, and a growing distance from them. I see men who feel unappreciated and threatened, distancing themselves from women they deem too demanding or unkind. Old, patriarchal system views shine through in systemic sentences like, "We take care of our women" and "Women belong in the home." I hear women saying, "I have to do it all. Cook, clean, raise the children, and have a career." The old servant mentality still shows up as working women find themselves trapped serving the needs of two full-time jobs, one in the home and one in the marketplace.

Sometimes men feel trapped too. When they do step into domestic roles, often there is pushback from their counterparts or from women who are accustomed to maintaining certain standards of beauty and cleanliness in the home—old gender standards that were expected of them. "He just can't seem to do it right," they complain. "If I want something done properly, I have to do it myself." Instead of looking at what needs to stop, start, and change, women are hard on men and even harder on themselves, perpetuating ancient patterns in systemic sentences like: "I don't need a man" or "Men are never there when you need them."

Creating sides solves nothing. It's time to see the good, acknowledge it, and give what's no longer relevant a place of wisdom rather than try to exclude it. Why? Because systemically, exclusions create patterns that expand and repeat. It's time we remember what each gender has sacrificed and gone through and brought to the table. The old gender system was useful for its time. That time is no longer. Now we need to examine the current gender system and its inhabitants mindfully and appreciatively and build from a place of higher, inclusive understanding.

NATIONALISM

Nationalism is defined as an identification with one's own nation or group and support for its interests. Taken to its highest potential, we can see a nation rise by pulling together for a common cause, as most Western nations did during World War II. Taken to the other extreme, nationalism can divide by creating exclusion and exclusivity amongst its citizens, as Nazi Germany did in the 1930s, elevating the blond, blue-eyed Aryan to heights of supremacy while condemning and destroying whole populations that didn't conform to that ideal.

Any time one group of people perceives themselves as better and more entitled than other groups, the others become victimized and angry. When this happens under the auspices of national identity, it has additional power, creating a vast blind spot where we no longer really see ourselves or the "other" we have created. We lose our humanity and create imbalance in all three principles in the system, creating exclusionary belonging, a sense of bigness or smallness, and a desire to take or receive without appropriate balance.

The negative nationalism meta pattern promotes national interests at the expense of other nations' well-being. Other countries are seen as harmful, threatening, or inferior. Political slogans drive rallies and then become systemic sentences: "Make Britain Great Again." "Better dead than Red." And, of course, Hitler's "One people, one empire, one leader."

When a nation starts following the individual rather than its government, the whole country's system is out of order and division ensues. Rules become tighter for some in order to control opposition. Foreigners are seen as a threat and often harassed and told they don't belong anymore. This often leads to the rise of dictatorships and eventual genocides until the system is corrected and the citizenry, once again, sees the greater truth that all belong and that connection is important for growth.

Negative nationalism makes enemies of any who dare to oppose the leader's goals and ideologies. If an internal correction isn't made, this can lead to another meta pattern: war.

WAR

War is a huge meta pattern with a number of survival patterns that arise from it. Systemically, I see its stark effects on clients and their families. Just like any other system, war has permissible behaviors and rules that involve seeing and doing things that are completely unacceptable in our regular, day-to-day lives. Soldiers are ruthlessly trained to break the most fundamental of all social codes: Thou shalt not kill.

In war, participants are stretched, tested, and reshaped by a system far bigger than them as individuals. The problem is, when soldiers return to civilian life, they are not the same people they once were. They have been immersed in a system diametrically opposed to normal civilian life and are now split between the two. But none of that is acknowledged. They are not offboarded from the war meta pattern and onboarded back into civilian systems in a conscious, systemic way. They are expected to easily transition from being trained killers who have done and seen unspeakable horrors, directly into being tender lovers and spouses and parents once more—usually within a matter of days or weeks.

With no exit strategy from one system to the other, they frequently find themselves feeling lost, abandoned, incomplete, and confused. "Homeless vets"—the moniker is apt and reflects what has happened to them. They are still "over there." Until they can be brought back home intact and a new purpose can be established, they are literally stuck between two worlds.

Veterans suffer in highly individualistic ways, and war affects each person differently depending on the family system in which he or she grew up. If it was a peaceful family system, the soldier may be more deeply affected than a soldier who grew up surrounded by conflict. The solution is to allow both the meta pattern of war and the meta pattern of peace to have their place in a way that does not overwhelm one or the other. War will always be a part of the soldier, but peace can be, too.

In systemic work and constellations, exploring what happened and being able to give each piece its place and purpose can bring about a much-needed settling. Constellations often allow just enough distance for people who have returned from war to be able to see in 3D what happened, addressing the ones who were lost, the ones who were hurt, and the ones who hurt them, making sense of harrowing events and resolving them in a way that brings peace and an ability to reintegrate purposefully into society.

RELIGION

Religion, an age-old driver of war and a distinct designator of who does and doesn't belong, is another major meta pattern. Just listen to the systemic language of religion and the actions it fosters. "We are God's chosen ones! Kill the infidels!" is a cry that fits just about any radical religious sect anywhere in the world.

There's a reason we're taught not to talk about religion or politics in polite society. Both are defined by powerful ideologies that shape our thinking, feeling, and conduct. Religious beliefs are deep and emotionally visceral. What starts out as practical codes of conduct that can guide humanity along a path of growth and personal evolution often ends up as fanatical rules and moral precepts that must be followed or else dire consequences will ensue. There's a big difference between "Thou shalt not covet thy neighbor's wife" and "Believe or burn in Hell for all eternity." One shows us how to live a more peace-filled existence. The other commands agreement and membership through fear.

All too often religion has us focusing on absolutes and doom and not on the miracles that right thinking can produce, moving us through life in a healthy way. Focusing on self-righteousness and separation, factionalism, noble suffering, and guilt, we miss the path to peace and unity that the remarkable founders of all our major world religions showed us in an attempt to bring us together beyond suffering and division. Unfortunately, we obsess over how their teachings are different instead of realizing how much they are the same. And then we go to war over the differences.

Religion is a meta pattern that guides people's every move and choice—often at great cost—until it can be understood and expanded into a healthy, elevating, transformative teaching system or set down with respect and another more inclusive, loving pattern can be adopted.

BEING "ONLY HUMAN"

This may sound strange, but the belief that we are "only human" is a powerful meta pattern closely aligned with religion that keeps us small, meek, and underdeveloped. Globally, we have been taught to think of humanity as weak, corrupt, and irredeemable. And we keep living down to these low expectations and possibilities.

All systems evolve—that is their mandate—and the human system is not exempt from this. Yet how many times have you heard the systemic sentence, "I'm only human!" as if that were an excuse for being limited, small, and petty? When we argue for our limitations, we are sure of only one thing: we stay limited.

When I talk about going beyond the meta pattern of being human, I'm not talking about falsely building up one's ego and self-esteem. I'm talking about growing up and moving out of the lower emotions of the ego—jealousy, greed, anger, judgment, comparison, and fear, which are driven by survival and neediness—into the higher emotions of love, compassion, understanding, inclusion, kindness, respect, appreciation, and gratitude. I'm talking about the elevated side of our language that we aren't really taught.

These higher emotions give us wings. They are the sign that we have indeed grown up, broken out of the meta pattern of being "only human" and expecting to be rescued and admired for our suffering, and are finally living up to our divine potential and taking responsibility for our lives.

POLITICS

"Vote like your life depends on it!" is not just a catch phrase. Our politics can define and drive our lives, and seldom is space created for mutual benefit and concern. Generally, the party whose policies and beliefs are perceived to support our self-interests and survival is the party we follow. Like religions, political parties are always in opposition. The "haves" support legislation that bolsters their financial position. The "have nots" vote the other way. Both sides feel threatened by the other and fiercely attack one another. Neither learns from the other.

Like religious affiliation, party alliances run generations deep. Many people don't vote with their present and future minds; they vote from their system's history. In an attempt to prove their parents right and love them, children often vote the way of the family. If someone dares to think differently, this can cause bitter division. The party must be supported no matter how harmful its current policies are. Thus, we see bad political choices made blindly against the clear best interests of a nation or group simply in order for the system or party to survive.

In some multi-tribal African countries, it doesn't matter how much you hate the tribal chief; you vote for the tribe you were born into. The idea of voting any other way is unthinkable. Some leaders go so far as to slaughter their opposition. Everyone knows they are wrong, yet no one dares to vote any other way. In the West, our leaders may not slaughter each other physically, but they slaughter and defame each other verbally in the press. But that's just the business of politics, which is filled with clashing agendas and constant efforts to "get what's ours."

Peoples' political backgrounds are easy to spot. Those with communist roots in the "old country" can present as generations of people who are afraid to open their mouths. Systemic sentences like, "The walls have ears" and "The tallest trees get chopped down" are commonly spoken. In America, slogans like, "The elephant works, the donkey kicks" reveal a conservative view and pride in a tough work ethic. "By the people, for the people" reveals a more liberal view.

As a meta pattern, if a political party or system sticks to blind loyalty and the old ways of opposition instead of evolving into a system built on cooperation, it can devolve into anarchy, dictatorship, and division. It returns to its past instead of creating its future. The way forward is to find a more inclusive, mutually beneficial way than opposition and "better than."

RACISM AND GENOCIDE

"I am better than you." This meta pattern flows from both religion and politics, and it's all about fear of loss of status and wealth. "I am better than you because of my genetics and thus entitled to rule over you." "I am better than you because my skin is lighter or darker." "I am better than you because my God is the real God." "I am better than you because my political system is the right system for everyone." During the Holocaust, if you didn't have blue eyes and blond hair, you would be sent to the camps. In Rwanda, you could be killed for having the wrong nose shape.

Racism occurs when a self-righteous system judges another ethnic group as "less than," justifying all sorts of despicable acts and choices. Devaluation moves toward marginalization that develops into segregation that results in social and economic tyrannies, right on down to dehumanization and slavery. Influenced by the larger system, smaller systems end up doing, thinking, saying, and experiencing the unspeakable.

The eventual result can be genocide, which occurs when the self-righteous system—usually under the spell of an unusually charismatic leader and in fear of their own defeat or exclusion—takes over the surrounding systems. People find themselves caught up in a frenzy of political or religious identification, slaughtering others for what appear to be perfectly logical reasons based on propaganda they are fed by leaders with their own selfish agendas, until they open their eyes, see how they're being used, and recognize the terrible things they're doing in the name of God or some petty despot.

When we boil meta patterns down, including genocide, we often see how they start with a single personality or a group representing patterns that need to be seen, expressed, or completed. We need look no further than Adolf Hitler for an example.

Hitler's father, Alois Hitler, was believed to be the unacknowledged illegitimate son of a wealthy Jewish merchant. Obsessed with the glory of military life, he wore a uniform and constantly abused his son Adolf until he died when the boy was fourteen, setting in motion a child's twisted hatred of Jews and a desire for military power that drew the whole world into a conflagration of horror. From a systemic point of view, if Hitler were a client, we might wonder if he unconsciously took on his father's pain: "For my dad, who wasn't acknowledged by the Jews, I will destroy them. No one will ever put my family (my nation) in that position again."

Sometimes the patterns of genocide run generations deep and nations wide. Children of Holocaust survivors frequently struggle to thrive in unconscious loyalty to their ancestors' suffering and abuse. Equally, children of the perpetrators can struggle to thrive because they are riddled by guilt over what their ancestors did. We keep the patterns of both victim and oppressor alive, passing them on to generations after us.

SLAVERY

Slavery is an example of a victim-oppressor meta pattern that is well documented yet has not been explored with curiosity rather than judgment. Within the meta pattern of slavery, *only certain patterns are allowed to be made visible* while others are buried. In this pattern, enslaved people are allowed to be seen only as victims rather than as human beings with infinite potential. Enslavers are allowed to be seen only as evil, and anything decent they did is ignored. I find this part of history important to address because *the nature of systems is that that which is suppressed and unacknowledged keeps repeating and expanding.*

Nothing can justify slavery, and we need to acknowledge all the terrible things that have happened, especially the meta patterns inherent in slavery, but we also need to realize that some strengths were created here too. The meta patterns of victims-oppressors continue to repeat through countless generations. Unless both sides do this work, heal trauma, and accept the trauma that was caused, we will continue to see the division and systemic imbalance.

FAMINES AND PANDEMICS

I talked earlier about the effects of the Dutch Hunger Winter and how that season of starvation affected later generations, showing up in anxiety disorders, disordered eating, and obesity. There hasn't been much studied about the generational effects of the 1918 influenza epidemic, and though it's too early to know how the current COVID-19 pandemic will affect future generations, there will, undoubtedly, be meta pattern impacts because the whole world has been drastically affected.

We're already seeing issues of racism, ideology, and culturism show up, with disadvantaged populations the most negatively impacted. Individual freedom is being demanded at the cost of many or restricted in favor of global cooperation. Denial is being countered by blame. We're seeing a disease being politicized, with science pitted against conspiracy theories and governments pitted against individuals. Certain sectors of the population are blaming others. Some people want to annihilate those who come from the country where this virus was first detected.

Separation in the form of social distancing is fracturing families and friends, schools, neighborhoods, and communities so that they can survive. A whole new way to work and operate business is developing. Travel is changing. The planet was momentarily given environmental respite. Adaptation and innovations are rampant. Outdated infrastructures, such as our health-care system, are being recognized as such.

The changes are enormous and global and sure to be with us for a long time to come, and of course so are the opportunities.

THE SYSTEMIC SLEEP OF "DOING OKAY"

There are lots of meta patterns in play within all of us. Some, like the ones detailed here, are obvious. Others, like patterns of hierarchy, structure, and control within language, etiquette, dress codes, education, literacy, and the immigrant experience, are not so obvious. However, before I close this chapter, I do want to mention one more major limiting pattern: the meta pattern of "doing okay."

When our lives are relatively okay, there is a strong tendency to fall into complacency and succumb to the systemic trance. It's just human nature. Our current systemic trance of "okay" includes stress and boredom, which are now a way of life—a set of habitual neural pathways in the brain that are instinctive for us. Keeping the dreary and repetitive but well-paying nine-to-five job, taking the same route to work every day, going to the bar on Saturday nights, eating out on Taco Tuesdays, watching TV, taking out the garbage. We trudge wearily through the week, then race through the weekends before getting ready to do it all over again.

We go along with what the systems dictate, do okay, have a relatively good life, don't rock the boat, and then . . . it's over. When we do rise up in rebellion against the complacency and boredom and wish for something more, we're often told to keep our feet on the ground, put our shoulder to the wheel and our nose to the grindstone. Somebody says, "Working on the assembly line was good enough for your father. It should be good enough for you." We're told that dreaming won't get us anywhere.

That is NOT true.

If there is anything you have learned so far, I hope it is that whatever your life is like now, it can always be more and change for the better because *you* can change. When we allow ourselves to want more and set up goals for ourselves and do everything we can to achieve them, we tap into another meta pattern available to us all called "wanting more, being more, having more."

A wonderful life doesn't just happen, especially considering all the systemic patterns that can hold us back. But once we see the old patterns, own them, give them a place to rest in our system, and start to dream—once we create the thoughts, feelings, actions, patterns, and mindsets for the dream to unfold—we're on our way!

Systemic Steppingstone #15: Dealing with Meta Patterns

Identifying meta patterns can be useful as you consider your own limitations, obstacles, desires, and evolution. They are key to recognizing both the places you get stuck and the ways you can elevate yourself. Here are a few things to ask yourself.

- Do you find yourself with strong opinions about other genders? How are the genders treated in your family system or place of business? Do you find yourself ranting against one gender versus another, or do you see a place for all?

- Think about your country of origin and the ways you think, act, dress, speak, eat, treat money, have relationships, act professionally, celebrate, and even grieve. Say to yourself: "As a citizen of _____ (America, or whatever your country of origin is), we _____" and fill in the blanks. If you stick with it, you will uncover a fascinating list of systemic sentences and rules you live by.

- Was anybody in your genetic lineage impacted by war, famine, immigration, financial disasters like the Great Depression, acts of terrorism, pandemics? Were they part of a great war?

- Was anybody in your genetic lineage part of an ethnic group with highly specific views of any kind?

- Are there victims or perpetrators in your system? Hidden secrets?

- Are you a descendent of a culture or country in which there was an ethnic cleansing? Which side of that do you represent? Do you find yourself excluding others, or are you a champion for diversity and inclusion? Do you carry the guilt or shame of the ones who came before you? Or do you pay it forward by being the change?

- What is asking to grow through you? In a world torn apart by differences of opinion, what can you do to enable healthy change?

Meta patterns are simply clues to understanding how you may be asleep and what to do to wake up. In light of the answers to the above questions, ask yourself:

- Where is my deepest frustration, limitation, or stuck-ness?

- What is the big meta pattern that has created a taboo or frustration that is limiting me? What is the rule I cannot break to get to where I want to be?

- What do I tell myself about that, and what do I make it mean about me/others?

- Now, what do I really want? (Your escape from the meta pattern lies in your dream.)

- What can I tell myself about the dream that is bigger than the meta pattern stopping me? What new thought will inspire me?

- How can I feel jazzed to the max in a way that drives me forward?

- What higher thoughts, emotions, and actions will lock in this new direction?

Remember: when you see the meta patterns and the history driving your life, don't be discouraged. Get excited. *Every single thing your ancestors did culminated in this moment in time when you can pivot and change.* We are all here to serve one another. Knowing this is higher learning.

PART IV

THE TREASURE
OF HUMAN
POTENTIAL

Building Beyond
Perceived Limits

CHAPTER 12

MINING YOUR RELATIONSHIP DNA

Personal Relationships

Relationships are hotbeds of systemic patterns, and how we relate directly impacts our quality of life. Our patterns of relating can be demonstrated to be generationally transmitted both in family and organizational systems, showing that *our patterns of relationships are often not ours.* We faithfully reproduce repetitive relationship responses to repetitive stimuli. It's not us and the person who is with us in relationship, but rather our respective family systems and their perpetuating patterns. Our destiny, should we choose it, is to move beyond limiting patterns and create something new and more robust.

Relationships are the keys to success, flexibility, growth, leadership, deep inner understanding, fulfillment, and happiness. Whenever you feel lost, trapped, stuck, resentful, angry, fearful, or diminished in a relationship, you are likely perpetuating a multigenerational relationship pattern in your family system at your cost, which serves neither you nor the system. An angry or dismissive parent can hinder a child's self-esteem, and I hear so many clients hanging onto how their parents affected them. But there comes a point where *you* have to choose who you want to be and how you want to relate. Blaming the parent who is also a person in a system keeps you from growing. Stop!

Good relationships develop strong patterns of coping and capability. They teach you more about who you are in the world and how to keep your heart open, your gut relaxed, and your brain switched on. Healthy relationships teach you all three of the principles in systemic work (chapter 1): how to belong in a way that enriches you, how to fully occupy your place and celebrate the place of others, and how to give but also receive. In other words, a good relationship can teach you how to live a fulfilled life.

When you begin to relate fearlessly and happily and feel and radiate a heightened version of yourself, you lay down new neural pathways, truths, feelings, emotions, and outcomes. Reinforced, these become richer ways of relating and collaborating with a profound sense of purpose, direction, and fulfillment. Life becomes a whole lot easier to navigate when you are strong in your personal relationships. You have a full-on team at your disposal—people who have what you need, who can point you in the right directions and enhance your experience of the world and the ways you operate in it.

Systemic Steppingstone #16: Relationship Check-In

To start the journey of creating strong relationships, look at the relationships in your life that are and aren't working. Write down the names of two important people in your life and describe the relationship you have with each.

For the relationships that aren't working, are they reflecting a pattern from your current system? From another generation? Or did you start the pattern? What events taught you how to relate in this unsatisfying way? What did you tell yourself about those events, and what did you make them mean? Is it the truth? Or is it *your* truth?

What systemic sentences do you have that define those limiting relationships? "I always feel unworthy. I always mess things up. I am not appreciated." Are these sentences part of your family system? Explore where they came from and notice your frustrations and your dreams. The frustrations show you the patterns that need to stop, and the dreams and desires indicate the pattern that needs to start.

Notice the kinds of people you hang around with. Notice the ones to whom you are loyal but who don't elevate you as a person. Look at the limiting systemic sentences that govern those relationships: "I'm not good enough, rich enough, smart enough, funny enough." For you to move ahead and grow, find relationships in which you dare to be more, think higher, and be happier. This may take you out of your family system comfort zone, but it's your next step. It doesn't mean you exclude your family system. It simply means you are the one to change the pattern.

Be aware of what lights you up or changes your thinking positively and go there. I was the shy, kind, good kid (nerd) who seldom spoke out in company until I took up dancing and overheard a trainer working with a bunch of new instructors. He said: "Remember, most people are even shyer than you are." It stuck. I knew how to be kind to shy people! One sentence and I unleashed an entirely new way of relating because I allowed a new truth in and fed it.

THE THREE PRINCIPLES AND RELATIONSHIP

In systemic work and constellations, being unable to belong and feeling out of order or balance of give and receive can bring woe to you and your relationships. The perceived inability to belong to your family system (which is literally not possible—we each inherently have a place in our family system) can put you at risk of feeling unable to belong in other relationships. Sometimes the exclusion is tied to an identification with someone else in the system who was excluded, and the solution is to give both that one and yourself a place. Excluding others is also a mode of not belonging, and those whom you exclude will show up in other forms in your system. We are here to learn from one another, and to do that, we need to acknowledge the place of those with whom we struggle. This allows the system to relax and us to learn.

Being out of order is another scenario that may indicate exclusions of missing members. When you are out of order in relationships, you do not know from whom to receive and to whom you should give. If you are metaphorically too big—shouldering the burden, always carrying the weight—others may struggle to connect with you. If you are too small and don't take your full place, you may not show up in ways that let others see you.

Sometimes the balance of give and receive seems inevitably inequitable. For example, how can a child balance the care they receive from their parents? The answer is that what we cannot pay back we can always pay forward to our own children and the community around us.

SOME WAYS WE CREATE LIMITED AND FAILED RELATIONSHIPS

The ways we create limitations and failures in our relationships are often based on issues with Mom or Dad, their relationship issues or those of ancestors further back. Our limitations and failures can also be based on events in our own line of siblings or our own life in response to a significant event. For the most part, I'm going to focus on parental dynamics since they are so influential. Each of these patterns or dynamics could be a book on its own, but for now I just want to give you a glimpse of what can get you into trouble and how to succeed instead.

Rejection of the Mother Figure

Our relationship with our mother begins before birth. Life flows through her to you. She may not be able to keep you or be there the way you like, but she is the one who brought you into the world. She is your very first and primary relationship.

Rejection of Mom is rejection of life and flow, and you may find both missing in your personal and business relationships. We also know that when we exclude something, as patterns are wont to do, they may show up in or around us. Ways you might notice this are systemic sentences, feelings, language, and actions you habitually say or engage in. Here are some examples of systemic "mother issue" sentences and their results.

Sentence	Result or Conclusion
She doesn't love me.	There's something wrong with me.
She's not there for me.	I become super independent and/or become ill or collapse.
It's always about her.	I have no idea who I am.
She doesn't take care of me.	I am big. I may eat a lot; I may neglect myself in other ways too.
She doesn't see me.	It's all my fault. I am not good enough to be part of a relationship.
I'm always the responsible one.	I have no support and no one to lean on. There's no one there for me.
She doesn't show her affection for me.	I'm always the affectionate one. I give all the time, and I don't know how to receive.
Mom is mean and unkind.	I am withdrawn and poorly resourced, or I am super kind and generous to compensate.
She intimidates me.	She takes my place and hers. I can't find my own place.
I am afraid of her.	All of the women in my family are afraid of their mothers. None of us can connect.
I don't trust her.	I don't know how to receive, flow, love, or birth things.
All she does is take.	I keep giving in hopes of her seeing I also have needs.

Ask yourself how much sentences like these populate your relationships. If you think you've escaped Mom, look at her relationships, and then notice the ways yours mimic hers. Write down the systemic sentences you hear from Mom and see how those shape your relationships too.

How you relate to your mother often carries the tone of how you are toward your partner or groups around you. A distant mom can equal an overly self-sufficient you, which can create a problem for you when it comes to connecting and letting others in. When you are in good standing with Mom, you tend to make strong, healthy relationships. If you cannot connect to her easily, you may find yourself connecting to more painful patterns. *I cannot stress enough how unconsciously loyal we are to our family system even when we consciously don't want to be.* And it's all because what lies there is unseen and unresolved. If you cannot connect overtly, you *will* connect covertly. We are always seeking a way to belong, even when we think we don't want to belong.

As a woman, if you are thinking about the mother you may become, you don't want to become what you reject. If you reject your mother, you may also find it difficult to navigate the professional world, becoming a daddy's girl, unable to take your full place, or struggle to interact with female colleagues. As a man, think about the ways your rejection of your mother may influence your children's relationship with their mother and then your relationship with your children as future mothers.

I know it's easy to say, "Don't reject your mother!" when I haven't met *yours*. But here's the thing: *systems don't care.* There is always something you can take from your mother, and if all it is is life itself, the color of her eyes, her hair—then take that fully and generate a sense of gratitude for it. What you can take, you can turn into gold. Giving her a place in your heart and conscious awareness doesn't mean she has to move in next door!

Rejection of the Father Figure

Dad introduces you to the world and shows you what is possible. Your very existence began with your father. If he wasn't present at the moment it counted, you wouldn't be here. Just like your mother, he is the holder of many clues to who you are, are not, and may become. When you reject him, you deny yourself access to the clues that could point you toward the life you want.

Here are some "father issue" systemic sentences you might hear, and some of the automatic responses to them:

Sentence	Result or Conclusion
He doesn't love me.	Therefore, I reject him first.
He's not there for me.	I will prove myself to him or feel like a failure.
It's always about him.	I have no idea who I am.
He doesn't take care of me.	I will look for other men to do so.
He doesn't see me.	I will do anything to prove I'm worthy of being seen.
I'm always the responsible one.	I surround myself with or hire people who play small, and I try to make them big (take their full place). If they can have their place, I can have mine.
He never shows his affection for me.	I always have to be the affectionate one. I come across as needy.
Dad is mean and unkind.	I perpetually feel as if I've done something wrong.
He frightens me.	All men frighten, annoy, or anger me.
I don't trust him.	I have difficulty forming relationships with men.
All he does is boss people around.	I am always smaller around men, or I become a bully too.

Ask yourself how much sentences like these populate your relationships with men. The way we relate to men and the world around us, especially in the business world, begins with our fathers. When Dad is a strong, healthy figure in our lives, daughters relate happily to men, and sons often emulate their fathers.

If we look at the multigenerational patterns of the father, we notice that how we fare in the world, especially in the professional world, is often modeled on our relationships with our fathers and the way they take their place in the world. In personal relationships, when a daughter rejects her father, she will still find a way to connect to him covertly—often by dating versions of him in an unconscious attempt to balance or complete the relationship she has rejected. Mistrust for men may dominate her personal landscape. As much as she might want a relationship, she may sabotage them unconsciously in the same ways she rejects her father. The rejection of Dad can extend to rejection of all male figures.

Sons who reject their fathers often struggle to embody their full male essence. There is a certain masculine strength and power missing in their bearing. The opposite is also true in that they may lack the capacity for male nurturing. What they won't receive may repeat in their children.

When Dad is not available physically or emotionally, this may result in children developing a drive for high visibility, proving that they are worthy of being seen, in an unconscious attempt to get Dad to see them. Even though they consciously reject their fathers, the inner drive to connect exists. Children of absent fathers may also struggle to sense their worth, feeling like there is something wrong with them because Dad didn't choose them.

Dad is an important figure in our lives, present or absent. Traditionally and archetypally, he is an externalizing energy that goes after a goal or purpose. Be grateful to Dad for the drive and the desire to look for opportunities to maximize your position in the world. As with your mother, there is always something you can take and appreciate from your father, even if it is "just" life itself.

Unbalanced Parent-Child Relationships

When a parent looks first to their children for emotional support, treating them as friend and confidante, they place their children out of order and put a heavy burden on them to meet their needs. The child can now become the surrogate partner and may be encouraged to pick sides or hear inappropriate secrets about the other parent. When parents don't look to each other first for support, the children may try to be the superglue that keeps the family together.

At the same time, we sometimes forget that the relationship between parent and child is a two-way street. The relationship is not just for the parent to show up but truly an opportunity for children to practice their relationships skills and rise to their higher capabilities. When this balance is off, we may see demanding children who feel like they never get enough and exhausted parents who can't wait for the kids to go to college!

Identification with a Parent Who Failed at Relationships

Daughters are particularly susceptible to repeating their mother's patterns in relationships or conversely to rejecting the same by banishing any man who shows even a whiff of the perceived flaw(s) that Dad had. Sons are the same, following the pattern of Dad's mistrust of women.

There is a deep, unconscious loyalty that says, "Mom/Dad, so you don't have to suffer alone, I will fail at my relationships just like you did." In these situations, our unconscious loyalty to the system trumps our personal desire. Sometimes children are fortunate enough to look at their parents' relationships and know that they do not want to repeat those patterns and then choose something else. Thanks, Mom and Dad.

An Interrupted Bond

When a parent is absent from a young child's life for longer than a few days this break in the bond is often not the fault of the parent. But the deep shock and unconscious inner decision of the child is harsh and damaging: "Whenever I need someone, they are not there for me. Therefore, I do not trust relationships."

This deep inner "truth" can persist and stall other relationships right at the point of real engagement. Of course, it's not a truth; it's simply a decision unconsciously made by a child about an event that, over time, has led to their distrusting everybody.

Inequitable and Unkind Divorces

Divorces aren't pretty, and ugly divorces can cause all sorts of systemic mischief for the children—of both the current and subsequent partnership(s)—via systemic sentences, thoughts, and feelings that create unintended emotional DNA. Dynamics in an acrimonious divorce can include the following:

- The partner who earned more may feel entitled to take more.

- The one who earned less or stayed at home may find themselves resentful, having given up their own career possibilities and then been entitled to less.

- The one who takes more as well as the one who receives less both set up emotional DNA patterns for their children to follow.

- Parents who formerly showed little interest in their children now engage with them as a means to use them to further their own financial ends, or to control their former partner.

- Parents who disparage their former partner may find themselves in a bind if they remarry and have children. One of the children from the newer bond may try to come between husband and wife as a way to include the one who has been excluded. This child unconsciously knows to whom they owe their life—the one who moved out so their creation was a possibility.

- If the ex-partner is disparaged, the current partner knows they are at risk for the same happening to them.

- Children are given the burden of having to navigate two systems and create two ways to please their parents in order to feel safe.

- Children don't feel safe or cared for, sensing the underlying tensions, war, and lack of appreciation for the other parent from whom they received half of their emotional DNA.

- Children often vocalize their parents' unexpressed anger, thus putting themselves in the middle of what doesn't belong to them and then being out of place.

Other Damaging Relationship Dynamics

There are obviously many other dynamics that can affect personal relationships—financial irresponsibility, inequitable earning, the issue of a one-earner household where one partner elects to stay home and care for the children and household, the death of a child, miscarriage, abortion, adoption or adopting a child out, just to name a few. Here are some more commonly observed ones:

> **Betrayals and affairs.** Betrayals and affairs can limit relationships, setting up the exclusion of the one we supposedly love and also the exclusion of honesty, which shuts down trust. The betrayed partner may feel spurned or conversely saintly and over-forgiving. If the latter prevails, this puts them in the "one-up" superior position. The betrayer may feel guilty, small, angry, or entitled, which puts them in the "one-down" position. This can cause an imbalance in the system where the one who has caused the issue feels treated like a child and may go off to seek solace with someone else (another affair) who enables them to feel their weight as an adult again.
>
> Depending on inherent family patterns, we sometimes find generations of men leaving their families to "discover themselves" at roughly the same age that their fathers went missing. Affairs may also occur when a parent is missing and you keep looking for the missing one and cannot stay present with your partner. This has more to do with your family of origin and less to do with you as part of a couple.
>
> The solution for achieving balance systemically is to pay attention to what has happened and take it seriously. A period of time for thinking through and cooling off is helpful. It should be set by the one who has been wronged so when the two come together, a mindful discussion can be had and a balanced set of consequences declared. After the issue has been fully addressed and an agreement arrived at, it must be given its place in the partnership. The betrayal is not pulled out for a rehash during every argument. Here each must learn what pattern wants to rest for them and what pattern is ready to grow through them.

Atoning for hurting someone badly. People who have hurt someone badly often don't know what to do about it. They can't move on because it hasn't been resolved and the person they hurt hasn't let it go; they're stuck. The result is often an attitude of: "If you can't move on and I caused this, how dare I live a good life?" We turn into both victim and perpetrator, hurting ourselves in revenge for what we've done. Either that or we seek forgiveness, which can possibly hurt the victim again.

I see this in partners who have hurt each other, and sometimes in women who have had abortions or given children up for adoption. Sometimes those who have had abortions feel guilty and may suffer inwardly. The solution is to look at what happened squarely in the face, acknowledge the effects, and then ask what can be learned and make choices that bring peace and growth.

Try to see the pattern that is wanting to emerge. For example, "I will learn from what has happened here." This is a strength. When you see the pattern, that insight becomes a gift you can pay forward, bringing life to life. You learn and gain purpose instead of remaining stuck in a pattern of recrimination, remorse, and self-abuse.

Demeaning language. We've all done it. "Lazy men! Stupid women who can't drive! Those lying, cheating, stealing good-for-nothings." Stop and take a good, long look. Do you find yourself uttering disparaging language toward any person or group around you? Where did that come from? How is it limiting you? How can you possibly have an elevated, joyful, growth-producing relationship with meta sentences like these in your head?

When we find ourselves typecasting individuals and groups, this is a wonderful moment to hit the pause button. Not only are we demeaning someone else, but we are also excluding them and ourselves from belonging, because who would want to belong to a group that demeans others? By excluding people, all you're doing is limiting your relationships.

Remember, what you decide and say about others will determine how you relate to them and they to you.

WAYS TO DIVORCE SYSTEMICALLY

Sometimes parting ways is the healthiest path for a couple to take. When things don't go as planned and two people do decide to split, there are ways to divorce systemically that make it easier on both parents and their children and teach each the art of relationships post-divorce.

- What's between the two of you should stay between the two of you. It does not belong with your children. They are too small for that, and it puts them out of order and into the place of being too big or a surrogate spouse.

- Relationship patterns are being set here for your children. What do you want them to learn from you?

- Being able to name the gifts you received from the marriage gives the marriage a place of weight; it teaches children and the divorcing spouses to find what is good in relationships and enables them to look at what they will treasure and what they will do differently. A good debriefing facilitates growth for everyone.

- Acknowledging the gifts that each has brought to the marriage facilitates kindness and amicable separation.

- Explaining to the children that you will both be present means that the children don't have to split their loyalties; they can choose both parents.

- Realize that if you disparage the other parent, one of your children may form an unconscious loyalty with the excluded one and repeat the disliked pattern in an attempt to include the excluded parent. Understanding that each parent occupies the first place and will always occupy that place gives the parents their place and the subsequent partners their places. When each knows where they belong, there is no need for friction.

- Acknowledging the ex-spouse makes it safe for both the children and any subsequent partners.

- When each parent can look at what they loved about their spouse, they will recognize those qualities in their children. The same goes for what they see that is wrong in their spouses. They will find the same emerging in their children.

- When children see kindness during the separation, they are able to give each parent a place of balance in their heart, and it sets a good example of healthy relationships.

CREATING HEALTHY PARTNERSHIPS

Partners do well together when each one understands that they are different but equal. Each needs what the other has, and each has what the other needs. For this reason, partners often take us to the sites of our greatest wounds. They can show us our most vulnerable places and offer us the chance to explore and to turn weaknesses into strengths. They show us what is unresolved in our family system. Often what we don't work out with our parents we will try to work out with our partners.

Systemic weight is created when you build together as a couple, growing families or perhaps tackling projects that carry the weight of a family. Accumulating assets and building wealth together are also ways to connect. Engaging in activities that nurture your bodies and minds grows your relationship DNA. Sometimes, if only one person grows, the relationship dissolves because the one with wings needs to fly. When one is engaged in activities that bring growth, if the other cannot be involved in the same activity, it is wise to find a complementary outlet so that both bring dynamic growth to the unit. Being joyful together and also grieving together creates strength for couples and a safe haven for both. Playing together and co-creating goals, hopes, and dreams builds joy and resilience, grit and glue.

CREATING STRENGTH AND FULFILLMENT
IN ALL RELATIONSHIPS

You build a relationship consciously when you receive and give fully with a full heart. Each giving and receiving builds upon the other. Doing this, you cannot help but build relationships that are rich and rewarding. High-volume giving and receiving brings with it feelings of abundance, joy, being valued, and valuing in return. Joy like this doesn't just happen. It is the consequence of your willingness to increase love by needing and feeding relationships. You can lean in and be leaned upon, hold and be held.

Every person in your life brings their system to the table, and it helps to understand that and be able to look behind the person to the ones with whom they are connected in the greater flow of life. Honoring the fact that everyone belongs in multiple systems allows us to bring the fullness of who we are into our relationships, without defensiveness, for exploration and growth. When we regard each other with inclusive eyes, hearts, and minds, something entirely new is possible.

Your relationship DNA is one of the master keys to your personal transformation. Who you are in relationship to others tells you how you are with yourself. If you listen to what you are telling yourself and others and observe your patterns of relating, you will quickly find what's keeping you stuck and what's helping you vault ahead.

Systemic Steppingstone #17: Creating the Relationships You Want and Fixing the Ones That Seem Broken

Step one. *Believe* that you can have the relationships you want in both your personal and professional lives. It doesn't matter if the current state of the relationship is difficult or even broken. If you don't have at least the desire and the belief that it's possible to create or improve, you won't even try.

Step two. Be specific about what you *want*, not what you *need*. There is a difference. One has space for personal growth; the other connects you to old wounds.

Step three. Seek relationships with people who will help you grow and develop into a greater person. Sometimes that means healing broken connections;

other times it means cultivating new growth. Make sure your relationships serve your highest good, and make sure you bring your highest self into them. You want to be excited by them and in turn excite and elevate them. They are keys to a brighter future.

Step four. Make sure the relationships you invest in are balanced. Don't just give more or try harder when the other can't or doesn't reciprocate. If you are not *both* working on the relationship, look at your balance of give and receive and question the pattern you are creating.

Step five. Enjoy your relationships, build on them, and invest in them. Well-developed relationships are a launchpad for the incredible in your life. The more you put into them and expect of them, the more fulfilled you—and the others in your life—will be.

CHAPTER 13

MINING YOUR RELATIONSHIP DNA

Business Relationships

Our business relationships are based on our personal relationship patterns. Many times, we unconsciously migrate limiting patterns from our personal relationships to our professional life and then wonder why we struggle with our career. Peers may represent siblings. Authorities and seniors may represent parents—and we interact with all of them accordingly. Understanding your personal relationships and their effects enables you to transfer that same insight to building strong business relationships.

For some of us, developing good relationship DNA can feel almost impossible in our personal life and surroundings. But the universe is elegant and generous. There are other systems available to help us develop relationship skill sets, and the workplace is rich with opportunities to grow. In business you *have* to be good at the job, and you are *expected to succeed* in order to rise up. The mandate is to evolve. We are allowed and even encouraged to excel and be the bigger versions of ourselves, and that permission enables us to bypass limiting family system thoughts, feelings, and actions. It allows us to test different ways to relate. Sometimes what you learn in your career helps you resolve an issue in your personal life and vice versa, leapfrogging you forward in terms of success, growth, and fulfillment.

I had a client whose father had told him as a child that only extroverts attain top positions. Because Mateo understood himself to be an introvert, he determined early on that he was unlikely to succeed in the business world and should settle for a supporting role. Basically, he was doomed. Mateo shared that people trusted him and often wished he would speak out more. But in his culture (he was raised in Latin America), speaking out was regarded as rude, and he'd been raised to defer to his superiors at all times and at all costs.

When he realized his belief that introverts come second, which derived from his dad, was limiting his relationships with his business peers and seniors, he knew he had to give culture and business each their own space. After thinking it through, it dawned on him that he could use his introspective nature to observe, evaluate, and then speak out clearly and inspirationally when needed. He reframed his thoughts to accept that introverts can be thoughtful and insightful leaders. He also realized that his culturally inspired politeness enabled him to question and challenge people in ways that invited interaction rather than defensiveness. Talking to his father resolved yet another layer when his father explained that he had been referring to himself—not his son.

A limiting pattern is only limiting for as long as you let its shadow side prevail. There is always an upside waiting for you to discover and use. For Mateo it came down to reframing his inherited limiting language and flipping the taboos into strengths that served him and others.

GROWING YOURSELF GROWS YOUR BUSINESS RELATIONSHIPS TOO

Business relationships tend to operate broadly in two areas: transactional and transformational. The first gets you what you need and where you need to go with a simple give-and-receive dynamic. You give service and you receive compensation. However, it's when you unlock something called *discretionary* relationship DNA—a higher part of you that radiates passion, kindness, enthusiasm, love, joy, and happiness—in collaboration with business associates and customers that transformational shifts can be made that result in legendary careers.

As a more junior person, you are likely to operate within the space of transactional relationships. At the lower levels of business, you get to know who is important, who can assist you, and what you need to do to connect and move. It is often more about *who* you know than what you know. You give your skills and enthusiasm, and those around you give you attention and mentoring. Starting right here, if you begin to use your higher emotions to find what you love or appreciate about each person around you and their role, you will not only increase your capabilities but also grow your discretionary business *and* personal relationship DNA, which develops when you go the extra mile to create value and deeper connection. You give first by serving the needs of others, and in return you receive wisdom, mentoring, and lasting relationships. Visionary leaders are known for their ability to connect. They consciously develop that skill set.

When you access and express higher emotions in business, magic happens. You make work a pleasure and thus become the person that others seek out, work with, and invest in. Advancement is a natural result. This is a life hack of sorts that gives you an edge. When I work with corporate leaders, I ask them every time we meet, "Did you go the extra mile and make magic this week?" It's one of those life freebies that gets you further up the ladder of success. Good vibes cost you nothing, everybody benefits, and the additional payoff is that being enthusiastic and joyful feels good!

In business, when we say your network is your net worth, we're not kidding. People want to help each other and will do so if there is a perceived ROI—return on interaction. But transactional relationships can only take you so far. It's the transformational relationships that take you all the way and create fulfillment. To have those and to be the "go to" person people love to have on their team, you want to work on your history and multigenerational patterns and move beyond the perceived limitations of your current system and into joy.

Systemic Steppingstone #18:
Transactional vs. Transformational
Business Relationships

In business you want to make sure you are setting yourself up to elevate beyond transactional business relationships. You want to continuously open the doors to more transformational dynamics. For this steppingstone I want you to take stock of your business relationships and be aware of whether they are transactional or transformational. Be aware that people do business with *people*, not just their capabilities.

Think about your job, career, or calling. When did you choose the direction you are going in now? Can you remember the defining moment or event? Was it an event that happened to you, or did an influential figure impact you negatively or positively? Did you unconsciously choose a career that would include or exclude certain groups of people? For example, people who enter the health fields often see themselves as someone who helps others.

If you chose your job or career for positive reasons, you've got a head start on developing transformational relationships and discretionary relationship DNA. If you chose your line of work as a way to stay small or invisible in alignment with a limiting systemic program or to simply survive, chances are that your choice has set up patterns that keep you in transactional situations. Was the language of your thinking along the lines of: "Not much is possible for me, and in this job, I won't ever be asked to be too much"? Or did you think something like, "I have something to offer. I can make my mark and be seen here." Notice the difference?

Did you take a position because nothing else was available? Or to simply put food on the table? While there's nothing wrong with doing either, these kinds of choices can set up an empty relationship with yourself that affects your business relationships because the best of who you are isn't showing up. You're not engaged and therefore don't want to participate; you can't generate an abundance mindset that will bring you and those you work with good returns.

Look at what you learned about business relationships growing up. Notice how you've typecast yourself into certain roles, limitations, and possibilities. "I'm too shy. Nobody will listen to me. I'm a nerd; no one wants me around." What you tell yourself from your systemic past would be comical if it weren't for the fact that your perceived personal limits lock you down into an equally limited perception of your business potential.

Make a list of all your perceived business shortcomings and then list the ways they affect your business relationships. Now ask: Do you bring your full self to the table? Do you take an interest in others beyond their roles? Do you inspire and invite followership and support? What one signature piece could you add to all that you do in business?

Ever noticed how top performers add that one small thing that differentiates them from the pack? A follow-up note, fresh baked cookies in a new home, interest in their customers' families. They are always looking for just one thing that gives them their own professional voice. They are growing their business DNA. Now, how will you grow yours?

WORK AS OBLIGATION

A lot of people are trapped in what I call "promise careers." Something happens that changes them and ignites a commitment, they make a promise to act or relate or live in a certain way, and they see that promise as set in stone. Let's say you're swimming with your little sister, and she almost drowns. A local paramedic does CPR, seemingly bringing her back from the dead. You feel guilty because she was swimming in water too deep for her, and even though all your young life you've dreamed of being a marine biologist, you promise God that if she lives, you'll dedicate your life to saving others. She lives, and you become a paramedic and work unhappily ever after.

Promise careers can create either powerfully positive or dreadfully limiting relationship DNA patterns. If you made a promise to yourself or God or the universe that inspires you and has given you purpose, fulfillment, and success, wonderful! Nurture it with open eyes and heart. Build your systemic library positively. In other words, fill your mind with thoughts, feelings, and actions that support your promise in ways that make you happy. If you are fulfilling a promise at the cost of your happiness, your promise and your job are a burden, and it shows in the ways you interact with others— transactionally and dispiritedly instead of transformationally.

Anything you do purely from a place of obligation holds no possibility for you to reach your highest potential, which is truly your best service to the universe. Take a look at what you have promised and how it has limited or inspired you. Many successful executives looked at their hardworking or failing parents and internally promised to have more, do more, and be more. Whether you have strong business acumen in your family line or you find yourself repulsed or frightened by limited circumstances and determined to make a better life, you have the igniters in your family system to thank for steering you and getting you to move!

WHAT KIND OF LEADER OR ASSOCIATE ARE YOU?

There are some patterns that are worth exploring to see what kind of leader or follower you are. Once you know where you are on the chessboard, you can see the direction you want to take and begin looking at the moves that will elevate you. The wonderful thing about emotional DNA—in this case, business relationship DNA—is that it all begins with you. You have everything that you need to begin rewiring what's currently in place so that you can change and grow.

The whirlwind leader changes direction every time their associates gain traction or establish direction, praising and criticizing by turns. Associates are constantly unbalanced, exhausted, and demoralized. Often such a leader comes across as the savior when in fact they are simply solving the problems they created so no one will find out that they are an imposter or don't have all the skills they think they should. This may originate from their lack of belief in themselves, which translates to a lack of belief in others. This dynamic also can stem from either being out of order or unable to belong. When this kind of leader invests in their development as a leader or leaves, the whole company heaves a sigh of relief.

The hidden or invisible leader. When a leader cannot be easily identified in the company, doesn't make decisions quickly or easily, and often says they need "forty-eight hours to sleep on it," there may be someone behind them who's calling the shots—the hidden leader or gatekeeper, a spouse or a family member who has their ear. Associates can't form relationships with this leader or get direction from them because the one who has their ear is creating an out-of-order dynamic and an interruption in the flow in the company.

The parental leader shows up as the father or mother figure in the organization, often making others feel smaller and unable to show up fully in their own right. Associates may relate to such a leader more like children than employees. The biggest downside is that associates never get to experience their own potential and contribute to the organization in the big way they could.

The reluctant leader often starts a company to satisfy a dream. Their wiring is more that of a founder and less of a leader. They are interested in the company's products or mission; they don't really think about the growth of the company and don't wish to be a motivator or people grower. As such companies grow, it is not uncommon to find this leader handing over the reins to a formal CEO so that they can focus on the company itself.

The driving leader is results-oriented and may have come from a high-achieving family or, exactly the opposite, they may be the first in their family to rise. Both backgrounds often promote belonging by controlling. The problem here is that these leaders often expect associates to do as much as they do, and that's not feasible. The pay scale and the rewards are different, and so are the personal desires and expectations. The balance of give and receive can get off-kilter if the leader is unaware of this; if charisma is also absent, associates feel unappreciated and overworked and may leave.

The visionary leader shows associates that they belong, invites them to bring their best, acknowledges their performance, gives them a place, and asks for and receives the best. They often compensate well, have high ROI (return on interaction), and inspire loyalty and passion by taking others along on the journey and making them part of the excitement. They give of themselves and show that they care and that others matter.

Just as with leaders, associates have a number of patterns that can keep them stuck or elevate them. Here are just a few.

Fearful associates bring their own personal fear-based relationships to their place of business and act as if something in the company is fearful. When teams or groups are fearful, business relationships can't flow or flourish because such associates are too afraid to give their best. The environment doesn't feel safe for them to emerge. They do a job for a paycheck, never sure if they fully belong, constantly waiting to be axed. A quick way to know if this is a personal fear pattern or an organizational one is to determine if this pattern repeats specifically for this associate, in which case it belongs to them. If this pattern is prevalent among a larger number of people within the team or organization, then you want to look into a pattern within the organization for its source.

Bossy associates and leaders are systemic examples of being out of order. Quite often they are trying to put everyone into order because they cannot find their own place. Their sense is that if everyone takes their place then they, too, will know where they belong. Business relationships can be strained when people feel herded like cattle or told where and how to belong.

The rebel associate can be a valuable asset to any company. They may represent who or what is being excluded from the system. When I work with a company and a rebel shows up, we look at what may not be represented, valued, or appreciated and what needs to happen for that associate or team to settle down. One company had a team of rebels who were angry and combative. When we looked at their history, we realized that they were the company's founding team and had been sidelined in favor of a newer, more glamorous team. They were still the major breadwinners for the company but had less and less visibility. In fact, the team had been moved to another floor, away from the public. Not only was this a case of being put out of order and excluded, the balance of give and receive was also shot. The team didn't feel like they belonged at all. A simple acknowledgment at the next corporate meeting, along with new office space in the heart of the building, brought the internal conflict to a halt.

Engaged associates reflect a sense of belonging, a place (order), and a feeling that their needs are being met while they are serving the company. They see the company as a part of them. These business relationships have a high ROI. The associates feel wanted and needed and have a sense of purpose.

BUILDING A GREAT BUSINESS SYSTEMICALLY

When I first started working with organizations using a systemic lens, it wasn't much of a surprise to realize that businesses have personalities, organizational DNA, hidden patterns, and unconscious loyalties of their own. After all, they are made up of people and they serve and interact with people.

Things that are straightforward in families, like ranking (oldest to youngest), are more complex in organizations and carry tremendous weight. Ranking, I discovered, is aligned with the dominant systemic thread or mindset in the organization, which can be age, time in role, skill set, stakeholder capabilities, and many other criteria. If the dominant systemic sentence thread or mindset of a business isn't respected, new hires can inexplicably stall when they try to innovate or create change.

One young CEO hired by a firm in Canada ran smack into a brick wall with the company. She couldn't get anywhere until she realized the dominant mindset and systemic sentence of the company was, "We respect our elders. Elders are the ones with the wisdom and knowledge." So she went to each senior member, saying, "There are things here I don't know. Can you show me?" She gave them their place, the walls came down, and everyone could play.

Companies rise or die based upon their internal relationships. Transparency through the ups and downs leads to less speculation and more willingness on employees' part to help during tough times. Human potential, when recognized and developed, improves the bottom line. When companies invest in their associates, their external business relationships improve too. They develop a common language and a sense of belonging. Instead of "the company rules," the dynamic is "Our rules: we come together to make the rules, values, and vision."

WHAT LIMITS OR DESTROYS BUSINESS RELATIONSHIPS SYSTEMICALLY?

Relationships run business, not just skills. They enable collaboration and expansion. But when you encounter hidden patterns and unconscious loyalties, business relationships can stumble and fracture. There are a number of ways in which this can occur. Some stem from multigenerational patterns in the business itself, others from the personal patterns of the people within the business.

Partnerships are about order and balance of leadership. When one partner suddenly dominates the other, order is disturbed. There is a sense that one is the leader and the other is in a secondary space. The relationship is one-up and one-down, and the word "partner" becomes inaccurate. The dominant partner treats the other partner as though they were a child or have less value. Often this pattern originates in the dominant partner from having had to take on too much responsibility as a younger person. The dominant partner feels safest when they have control, just as they did growing up. This can destroy partner relationships because they don't know how to share the space and lean on others just as others lean on them. Often the other partner will seek an opportunity elsewhere that lets them grow through experiencing the frustrations and joys of being a full partner.

The child partner is the opposite. There is a part of them that cannot grow up and assume their full responsibility. They often have gatekeepers to protect them and disguise the fact that they can't be fully available as a leader. They may have the smarts but not the ability to form leader relationships with other partners or associates. Others have to clean up their messes or create direction when they can't or won't. They may have imposter syndrome, and the solution is to explore the fear that keeps them from connecting with others, reframing their imposter syndrome into pioneer syndrome, growing up and assuming their full place as a partner.

Parentification can also happen when a junior associate wants to parent the leader or others who are more senior than they are. Both are then out of order, and the flow is disturbed. Neither can rise to their full potential. The leader cannot take their full place and lead the company, and the junior member cannot receive the mentoring they need to succeed.

Triangulation is a well-known pattern with systemic roots that creates uneasy relationships and distance between partners, trapping more junior members who get caught in the crosshairs when partners use them, consciously or unconsciously, to create sides and strengthen their causes. The associate is then caught in the middle between the partners. The solution is for the associate to step away, leaving the struggle or conflict where it belongs—with the partners. Failure to do so frequently results in the more junior associate being accused of fomenting mischief or taking sides inappropriately and then being ousted.

Misaligned values, visions, and missions between partners can result in splits within the company as teams and associates align with their line managers and find themselves at odds with other teams and line managers. The solution here is to create one set of clearly codified and agreed upon values so all associates know how to relate and interact with one another.

Unclear communication around visions and goals creates tension among leaders and associates alike. Nobody knows how to belong or relate, tensions rise, and it detracts from the company's direction and results. Everyone is busy trying to decode the rules and the most powerful leadership lines so they feel safe. The clearer the vision and the goals, the more the nervous system of the organization can relax. Companies that have clear career paths, expectations, and direction tend to have happier associates and are more cohesive. Systemically, clearly defined roles, scopes of work, and parameters for projects mean each person knows where they belong, what is expected of them, and from whom they should receive and to whom they need to give.

Family-owned businesses often carry both family and organizational dynamics, and if the two are entangled—which they often are—the family patterns play out through clashing company teams, aka sibling rivalries. There is also the dynamic of family versus non-family employees, who can end up feeling and being treated like second-class citizens. If you look closely at the business, you can sometimes tell how the family is doing, who is aligned and who clashes, and navigate accordingly.

In conclusion, your business relationships are worth their weight in gold. No matter what position you hold, your relationships are sources of growth, healing, creativity, abundance, and fulfillment. The sooner you learn to relate well, the sooner you broaden your network. If you're going to be at work or engaged in a career for eight hours a day, it may as well be fun—and the responsibility to make it so lies in you: in your thoughts about those around you and your attitude toward your career and yourself as a professional.

Systemic Steppingstone #19:
Seeing Where You Are and
Getting to Where You Want to Be

The biggest key to growing your business relationship DNA or, for that matter, your emotional DNA, is to put down your assumptions, declarations, decisions, and theories about yourself, others, and relationships, and start completely new—preferably from a place of what you want to achieve.

Step 1. Let's look at the business ethic or systemic business mindset that currently defines you. What language do you use about your career and business? Pay attention to the sentences. Where did they come from? A parent, educator, influencer? How might you reframe them into sentences, patterns, and mindsets that serve you and surpass the limits of your system?

Typically, your business relationship DNA is based on old systemic sentences that have migrated from your family system to your career or business field either in collusion with or reaction to your family system. If it is already strong, build on it and take it to the next level. Find what differentiates you and discover your capabilities beyond your assumptions and systemic sentences. Always look for your own voice. That's your secret sauce. As I said before, it doesn't have to be loud or large, just pure you.

Look at where you struggle. Perhaps you are shy, impatient, abrupt, sarcastic, withdrawn, quiet. Where did that come from? Pick just one thing to change, find its alter ego, and invest in that. Work it until you find your unique way to flip it. That is your gold. Keep doing that with each of your struggle patterns one by one. They usually end up being your strengths in disguise.

Look at your level of ambition or lack thereof and ask, Where did this come from? Is it a multi-generational pattern? Was there an event that created it? Do you find yourself shutting down or shrinking when challenged, or do you use challenges as clues to opportunities for growth, exploration, engagement, and enhancing your ability to relate?

Step 2. Build better business relationships to get ahead. Look for the positive ways you relate to others. Perhaps you are a good listener, collaborator, teammate, slogger. Whatever it is, grow it with all your might and make that another differentiator for you. You are building your value. Be proud of it and champion it. Get superbly good at it. That is your gift. It might seem small to you, but it pays large dividends. Maximizing what you have and who you are is a universal freebie.

Learn to relate up as well as you relate peer to peer or peer to juniors. Develop a broad swathe of internal and external stakeholders.

If you don't know something, ask. If you do know something, share. If you shy away from either, ask yourself where *that* came from. Does it serve you? If not, then what small aspect of that tendency can you shift that allows you to move beyond your current bandwidth and capability? The one who leans in and engages bypasses limiting patterns, learns, grows their business DNA, and increases their opportunities.

Explore your frustrations around your work and your work relationships. If you are frustrated, chances are high that your business mindset is too small or you've outgrown your current role. Your irritability is telling you clearly that something wants to be completed so it can rest and something else is trying to emerge for you. Pay attention.

CHAPTER 14

WHERE IS YOUR BEST?

Your Success DNA

I f you take only one thing from this book, I hope it is the realization that it is your destiny to want more, expect more, and be more, and that transformation begins with daring to believe it's possible and going for it. Your destiny is to rise and shine from the inside out. To feel good about yourself and life. To relax and feel blessed and complete and always ready for more. Because *more* is what you are capable of and what you were born to create.

Truly, just growing up, learning, surviving, taking care of yourself and others—all those things are no mean feat. If you've accrued $10,000 in net assets—basically a well-used car, some furniture, and a TV—you are among the top 20 percent of the wealthiest people in the world. Just reading this far in this book means you've grown far beyond the vast majority of people on this planet. You've taken the ultimate step in life: you've accepted responsibility and realized that how far you take the game of life is entirely up to you.

In this technological, wired age, opportunities for success abound. Maddie Bradshaw made her first million by age thirteen turning bottlecaps into jewelry and gym locker decorations. Adam Hildreth of Leeds, UK, founded the social media platform Dubit at age fourteen. By age twenty-nine, he had a net worth of £24 million. What's next for them?

Success in material terms creates a whole lot of freedom, but money is not the entire story by a long shot. Wealthy clients come to me all the time because they are wanting more—they want to know how else they can be successful. They want meaningful adventures that will let them feel like they have made it as an authentic human being. They want to feel connected to life and other people, united with their lineage and the universe in profound and mystical ways. They come to me because they want to expand their definition of success and enjoy family, have a deeper purpose, be healthy, and above all feel good about their entire being.

I have a billionaire client, Ralph, who came to me saying he wanted success. When I asked what that meant to him, he said he'd been so busy making money to ensure that his family was safe, he'd not had time to enjoy or share it. Success for him meant being able to put down his computer, be with his family, and not feel guilty about not working eighteen hours a day. And yet, like so many driven people, he was afraid that if he stopped working it would all go away.

His father had been shamed by his inability to accumulate wealth, and Ralph had promised himself that he would never be shamed that way. Although his father had been the spark for change in the family systemic pattern of poverty, Ralph's accumulation of wealth had driven a wedge between them, and the connection Ralph yearned for wasn't possible. I pointed out that systemically when a child surpasses their parent, it can leave some parents feeling out of order and inadequate. I invited him to go to his father and say one simple sentence that we shaped from what he told me: "Because of you, Dad, . . . me."

The change in the relationship was remarkable. His father could celebrate the son he had given birth to and know that he had done something right. He could take his full place, and his son could take his own place and finally lay down the family burden of shame. The whole family is currently an inspiring example of service to the planet. Success is expanding its definitions through them as they all discover how to make magic with what they've created.

ONE STEP AT A TIME

Success means vastly different things to different people. It also means different things at different times and stages of life. So, the first step toward success is defining and redefining what it means to *you* now. For some it is safety, for others health, and for others success centers on career, spirituality, or relationships. Because we are so heavily programmed by social norms, it's inevitable that most people's first thoughts about success will involve money, material goods, and prestige. But everyone's definition is wonderfully unique. I had one client define success as having beautiful, fresh flowers in every room of her house all year round.

The other thing to realize is that no matter how quickly or easily "success" comes, it still arrives loaded with emotional DNA from prior generations. Unresolved patterns of failure imprinted on the family system can sabotage your success very quickly. The newspaper tabloids are full of stories about rising stars full of passion suddenly committing suicide or becoming drug addicts or losing their money. Readers scratch their heads and think, "Why did they do that? They had it all and blew it!"

Yes, they had it all, including unexamined systemic sentences and patterns that ensnared them in ancient history, overwhelming their fabulous lives, sabotaging their incredible futures, and telling them subconsciously why they weren't worthy. Until and unless all the old baggage is seen and resolved, many a successful launch and phenomenal career is destined to tank right at the point of achievement.

Systemic Steppingstone #20:
Reaching for Your Best

Write a one-page document defining what success means to you. (I suggest that you do not show this to others; it can be torn down by naysayers.) Set no limits. You'll know you've hit what real success means to you when you find yourself nodding and smiling like a Cheshire cat, feeling the entire world sparkle. Anything less won't cut it. Once you have that feeling, grow it! Don't ever let it go. That sparkly smiley feeling is your compass pointing you toward success. *Your* success.

Now look at your page and notice any resistance that comes up. Any Debbie Downer voices. To whom is that resistance to success tied? Who told you that you couldn't be successful? Who told you that what you wanted isn't what success is all about?

The page that you create is your own, very personal contract with and treasure map for your future self. No one else needs to know about it for now. One day it will be your story.

Success is about going beyond a limited vision of yourself one step at a time. It's about expansion. I remember when my mother, daughter, and I decided to take our first vacation in many years, we sat down and imagined where we wanted to go. We knew we wanted beach time, but our budget was tight, and all the systemic thoughts and feelings about why we shouldn't and couldn't take a vacation came up. "In our family we are frugal. We stay within our means. We build carefully and save for a rainy day." With these thoughts in mind, we limited our search to Florida beaches only. But the beaches we looked at just didn't do it for us, and so (daringly!) we took a chance and looked at some Caribbean beaches. To our shock we found many beautiful places that were affordable, even with the airfares. With one different thought, we'd gone beyond what we thought was possible and expanded our world!

Of course, then came the next set of negative success DNA thoughts, feelings, and actions. "What if this is a bad place?" we wondered. "What if it's a scam?" Worst of all came the thoughts, "What if we need the money before vacation time arrives? Can we get our money back?" It was only when we were finally there and had paid for it and it all worked out that our nervous systems started to relax. Then we started thinking about the next vacation. Excited, knowing our vacation limitation cycle had been broken, we pushed our vacation boundaries even further.

The same thing happened the first time I hosted an event at a large center. They asked for all sorts of deposits up front that put me at financial risk, and I was terrified. All the old "what if" and "you can't" thoughts came up, bringing stress and fear. But I knew those old voices. I was clear about the limiting systemic sentences in my head. I also had a clear vision of what success meant to me—helping large communities of people to disentangle their emotional DNA and create the best lives possible for themselves. That vision helped me focus on purpose, motivation, and success, cancelling out the impact of the old emotional DNA. I booked the center, and the event was a resounding success. Then I did it again, and then again. It took a long time to move out of fear and the "What are you thinking!" mindset. But step-by-step I did it, and with each step I pushed the boundaries a little further.

This steady, incremental approach to success works. If a dream sounds too far out of our bandwidth for us to accomplish, the weight of old systemic baggage can make us give up before we even start. But if our success goal is something we *deeply* desire, and we take the time to learn about our success DNA and then chunk our progress down into doable steps, no mountain is too high for us to climb!

PURPOSE AND THE SEVEN LEVELS OF SUCCESS

Success is directly tied to purpose, and purpose is tied to personal motivation. Purpose is the rocket fuel that blasts you past your negative systemic sentences and programming. The clearer and more embodied and inspiring your purpose, the greater the success. However, there are different kinds of purpose driven by different kinds of motivators.

Lowest level motivators are based in survival fears. "I must make a lot of money so I don't starve like my grandmother did." "I must succeed and get my kids out of this dangerous neighborhood!" There's nothing wrong with fear as a motivator and survival as a purpose. Sometimes it's just where we're at. But the more we taste success, the more we want to expand and see where else it can take us and what more we can create. Who can we become? Material drivers gradually transform into spiritual drivers as our consciousness expands. Love replaces fear as a motivator. We rise from a reactive/victim mindset to a creator mindset.

7 Levels of Success Through a Systemic Lens

Level	Unhealthy Motivations	Creator	Healthy Motivations
7	N/A	Service	I am in service. I understand the importance of success as a friend, ally, direction, and expansion. I am now as much teacher and mentor as student.
6	N/A	Impact	My family system is a welcome part of who I am. What used to hurt now illuminates and enlivens. I am success in positive action.
5	N/A	Coherence	Heart, head, and gut are open. I am in service to a larger community and agree to become the biggest me possible. My destiny, purpose, and adventure begin.
4	N/A	Transformation	I am open to more. Success is seeping into my DNA and invites me to be more. I take responsibility for my life and want to see where I can take it.
3	I am an imposter. People will find out.	Self-Esteem	Who I am matters; what I say counts.
2	I need to know I am okay and that I belong.	Relationship	I am learning to engage and give and receive to rise.
1	You failed and I will, too, just like all those before me.	Survival	Mom/dad/family members: I choose to succeed in ways you couldn't.

Victim

I talk about seven levels of systemic success DNA. No level is "better than" another level. Success DNA of course applies to any area of your life where you wish to achieve success. We need all the levels—some for support, some to help us build, others to attract and rise. As we examine the levels, you will likely notice that you identify with more than one. This is quite common. You are likely to find yourself on the lower levels when you are in survival mode and also when you are creating the base for your next step up. The higher levels tend to show up when we go into our creative space where limitations are fewer, until they eventually disappear. Depending on your beliefs and what you make them mean, your spiritual orientation may land you in different spaces as well.

As you read about the levels, notice what resonates or stirs up limiting thoughts for you. What or who stops you from imagining your highest good and happiness? What or who stops you from dreaming your dream? What do you tell yourself about success and purpose? Are you daunted by the very words?

Levels 1-3: Blind, Reactive, Closed, Survival-Based, Imposter Syndrome Success

At the first three levels of success, DNA is rooted in escaping failure and drudgery and a need to belong and be relevant; imposter syndrome is a motivator here as well. In these levels there can be a strong desire to do things differently, move ahead, build stakeholders, and create a compelling differentiator. Impatience and appetite are pronounced. There may be a robust vision but also a frustration with apparent limitations and a niggling fear of getting too big.

Unconsciously, the flavor of your success DNA is likely to be worthiness-oriented at these levels. Your thoughts, feelings, and actions tend to center around surviving, struggling, building, driving, and proving yourself. Here, survival *is* success. Feast and famine are common. Your perceived limitations can feel overwhelming. Drivers are mostly fear oriented, and relationships are often formed based on their usefulness. This is the beginning of your adventure. You are seeking your first grains of success, and you cultivate stakeholders and friends and learn to navigate other systems even as you are growing your own. Politics can feature quite prominently here. Who and what you know is important as these connections give you leverage.

Life can feel like a slog, a challenge, or an invitation (your attitude determines your experience). You may feel like you are constantly working to do enough to build a solid base, get your life together, and advance. Success at this level is a little scary. Self-doubts can be high. You fear your ability to attain success, and when you have it, you may fear its loss. The upside is that you may discover you are a great workhorse. You can become an expert, create a strong network, and position yourself to recognize and take advantage of opportunities. The downside is that you can suffer from burnout and be overwhelmed by all the negative stories you tell yourself. Operating at a level three, you may find yourself vacillating between feeling like you are an expert and an imposter. As you solidify at level three, feeling like you know a little more and have a little credibility, a restlessness creeps in. You know the life of slog and find yourself thinking, "There has got to be more to life than this."

Level 4: Success DNA Becomes Deeply Transformational and Purpose-Driven

Here, there is an insight that not only is success allowed, it's a natural part of your evolution. There is a sense that there is an adventure with your name on it. You begin to take full responsibility for your life and success. There is a sense that being a victim is no longer an option.

At level four you realize that success is not about struggle and survival but rather about accomplishment, personal challenge, and freedom. You begin to see success as the key to a more fulfilled life. It becomes intriguing and even exciting to challenge some of the limiting beliefs, mindsets, and feelings you hold about success. Instead of judging others and comparing yourself to those who appear to have more, you are curious and wonder what it might be like to have "that." You begin to wonder how it might be if you were to do something different. You start questioning your definition of success, wondering if more is possible, and you begin to listen to your inner voice for direction and inspiration.

Here you are curious and less defensive. You don't mind being wrong or not knowing. Those possibilities are no longer a threat to you. You simply want to learn. Your heart begins to open, and that makes way for the creative part of your brain to activate. You acknowledge the patterns that are part of you and begin exploring them for clues to the next levels you sense are waiting to emerge. You begin to see the world around you as filled with opportunity and possibility rather than oozing obstacles. At this level you also realize that who and what you are in life is nobody's fault, that blaming, shaming, and naming others only locks you into all the old patterns that have you stuck. You begin to realize that you are the captain of your own ship and start consciously identifying and breaking old patterns, mindfully creating new ones. Everything is shifting from fear based to heart centered, and you realize that you have always been living in a spiritual world. You acknowledge your systems and their gifts. You even understand the gifts in your limitations.

Levels 5-7: Openly Successful, Community Building, Heart-Centered, Service-Oriented Success

There is a clarity that your voice and contribution matter. The heart, head, and gut align, purpose emerges, and your highest vision for your life is now a possibility. Your own voice becomes important as you realize there's a chapter that only you can write. You create community. You are in service.

At level five you consciously agree to become the biggest version of yourself, which brings about cohesion, humility, and responsibility for creating a wonderful life. With this comes a sense of your own voice and also of your tribe—those to whom you may be of service. Your desires increase, asking more of you. Growing yourself becomes a priority. You understand that success is actually mystical, divine, and part of who you are. You know that success is energy: a living, flowing force just like love, health, and money. Your language shifts to the language of possibility, and you use it to shape a better, kinder world. You give thanks to success every day with an increasing appetite to experience more, recognizing that embodied experience is the doorway to deeper wisdom. Life is beautiful and awe-inspiring, and you model what is possible for others.

When you arrive at level six, you are an expression of the abundance of the universe in action, and making a difference is part of who you are. You have a unique voice, and you use it to move both yourself and others to higher levels of expression and choice. You integrate and honor the wisdom that all systems bring. You know how to give each its place as you make a difference in the world.

At level seven you are success in action and in service. Success is now an inherent part of who you are. You see cycles and patterns as continual invitations to evolve. You are a mentor of ever greater possibilities for others and yourself.

Many phenomenally successful people didn't necessarily mean to achieve great fame and fortune. They started out wanting to achieve safety and freedom. Those were the first drivers, and then, as they evolved along the way, they became more and more turned on to life's possibilities and their own potential. That urge, in turn, gradually expanded to include reaching out and helping others.

When I started my career, my life was about the family surviving. When my father was killed shortly after we moved to the United States, it was pretty much all on me, and life wasn't fun. I was in a strange country, terrified, with no support but the love of my family. I knew I wanted to be safe and free, and that drove me. But living from a desire for safety and freedom wasn't enough. It didn't feel much like success. Ultimately, I wanted to love what I did with all my heart. And then, along the way, I fell in love with the courageous clients around me and the incredible possibilities that systemic awakening and transformation offered them—and me! But it still didn't feel like I was a success until I could teach at a place I love (Walt Disney World) and start creating products that I knew would help others find their magic too.

That's when I started to understand what success fully looked like for me. It meant joy, love, laughter, community, transformation, and the biggest piece of all—higher purpose. When I realized the possibilities for large communities of people to create their best lives, which meant more people for me to interact with joyfully, the lights went on. *That* was the magic I had been looking for. That was my purpose. And with the arrival of my purpose, all the woes and excuses and fears vanished.

SUCCESSFUL FAILURE

Success is a habit. It is not a one-time thing. People who have a one-time success often find themselves restless and lost. They got there but don't know how, and they are scared they will lose it or never get there again, proving that what got them there was sheer luck, not skill. Which means even their success doesn't feel successful.

Systemic Steppingstone #21:
Breaking Limiting Cycles

As you contemplate the success you want in your life, know that where you are *now* is *not* an indicator of your future success. You may simply not have flipped the switch yet. In Systemic Steppingstone #20, you wrote down what success means to you. Now let's address the fears and limiting sentences you carry that stall the successes you desire.

Write down the scary, sad, or overwhelming sentences you have around success and failure. What horror stories do you tell yourself and then believe? "I can't do this. I'm not good enough, smart enough, connected enough, brave enough, _____ enough." Fill in the blank.

Write them all down. What have you made these sentences and stories mean about you and your success? Where in your life did you first become aware of failure? Was it a specific event? Did you witness someone else in your family fail? What did it look like? Who did it happen to, and what did you tell yourself about that? How is your failure similar to that original failure, and again, what have you made it mean? How is failure perceived in your family, culture, religion, country? Whose nightmares, U-turns, and limitations are you borrowing? How are they serving you? How are they holding you back? How much of your negative success DNA is really even yours?

Where do you feel that in your body? Your throat, chest, gut, arms, legs, teeth, eyes? Perhaps you are smack in the middle of your biggest "failure" right now. If so, all I can says is, "Well done." Failure tells you a lot about what you *don't* want success to look like, and that is a great clue to what you *do* want. Thank it for its presence and illumination.

Now that you have these sentences and insights, ask yourself, "What will allow me to put these feelings down? What would be more exciting than this? Am I ready to allow one new thought, feeling, and action to start changing the way I see myself and invest in that?"

PUTTING THE SUCCESS TRAIN IN MOTION

Success DNA can be boiled down to a few simple guidelines:

- Don't ever buy into the myth that desire is unhealthy. Every marvelous invention known to humanity was birthed out of deep want and absolute commitment. The bigger the desire, the bigger the appetite and the greater the potential. If you weren't allowed to want anything as a child, remember, that was then, this is now. Purpose and appetite will pull you past all your excuses and into your dream life.

- Don't judge what you want; *choose* what you want. In other words, say yes in your head, heart, and gut, and then invest in that want. Whether it's creating a business empire, teaching knitting, or exploring the world, if a goal fills your heart and soul, that's it. Don't settle for less, ever!

- Choose success without apology or guilt.

- Develop inner focus. Look for systemic patterns and sentences that are shaping your attitudes about success and desire. Choose the healthy ones, resolve the unhealthy ones, and move on.

- Cultivate the habit of higher emotions. They wire the brain for success.

- Acknowledge your family systems and their gifts. They are clues to your struggles and your destiny.

- If you achieve less than you desire, go at it again. Don't ever give up. You got part way. Now start from where you just ended. Commitment is everything.

- The highest success feels good, brings joy, and is ethical, kind, and grateful as you create and achieve it. To create it otherwise generates patterns that will leave you feeling empty and your system feeling burdened.

- Acknowledge even the smallest gains. Acknowledgment enables you to notice more opportunities for growth.

Finally, when you think about success, DO NOT THINK SMALL! Let what you deem success evolve. Let the ideas come. The more you relax and stop struggling to succeed and enjoy the creative process—the more you allow and appreciate the flowering inside you to occur—the easier and more joyfully things will flow. Love what you are doing. I cannot say that enough. Be excited about it even when it scares you. No matter who you are or where you are in your life right now, you *can* achieve success. You simply have to choose it with all your heart, and then go there.

CHAPTER 15

SHOW ME
THE MONEY!

Money DNA

I'm going to start this chapter with a statement that you might find startling: money is not a commodity. It is a *relationship*—it reflects your connection with abundance and flow, creativity and possibilities, power and potential. It also directly reflects your systemic language and thinking around having it or not.

Money is the single most desired and disdained object of all human creations because most of us only understand it in materialistic terms. Since ancient times, we have worshipped and despised it; lusted after and rejected it; judged, misunderstood, and misused it. A global meta force that funds war and peace, health and sickness, feast and famine, limitation and freedom, money separates the "haves" from the "have nots," forming the power base of individuals, corporations, and nations.

The strongest of task masters, money provides opportunities of every sort, teaching us many ways to grow and many ways to stagnate. Money stimulates and reveals our deepest fears and provides the means for realizing some of our greatest joys. With our tacit agreement and alignment, both individual and societal, money largely determines where and how we live and interact in our world. When our relationship with it is healthy, it supports us. When it is not, it seems to undermine our lives with a vengeance.

A symbol of flow and abundance, power and control, ease and graceful living, generosity, poverty, and suffering, no one can doubt its vital importance. Even when we turn our backs on it, it is still a powerful influence in our lives. Is it any wonder that money DNA is alive and active in all of us? As a part of our lives for thousands of years, money and our ancestors' relationship with it *must* affect us, shaping our future on a daily basis.

A TREASURE WE LOVE TO HATE

Would you disparage and revile a friend or a business partner who totally supported your growth, abundance, flow, possibilities, and opportunities? Of course not. Yet for many, it seems to be a mark of honor to disown money even while needing and wanting to enjoy it. It is seldom treated as a friend. When I realized there was nothing in my life that had the same kind of negative charge around it, I finally acknowledged that there is more to money than just pieces of paper or numbers in a bank account.

At age three, I loved gathering seeds from a canna plant in our yard. I realized that if I picked them up, my mother could plant more, and then they would make more flowers and then more seeds, and so on until we had fields of flowers. I had a sense of what abundance could do and how it might expand beauty. It was my first interaction with a currency of sorts.

At age five, I started picking up empty bottles and bottle tops along the roadsides for money. I remember imagining all the things I could do if I had a lot of those coins the storekeeper kept giving me for the bottle returns. I wanted to figure out all sorts of ways for that flow to happen and to be able to have adventures I could share with others!

However, I was also accustomed to hearing that kindness, honesty, and money didn't go together. Because kindness and honesty were particularly important values for me, I subconsciously began to avoid money. Soon I had manifested the reality of the systemic sentence, "Don't be greedy." Instead of an abundance of coins, I had created the reality of "just enough."

As a young adult I went to a casino with some friends one evening. While I was holding a jar of coins for someone else along with my own jar of coins, I accidentally inserted three of *their* coins into a slot machine and hit a small jackpot—money my family *really* could have used at the time. Now, most people would simply have replaced the three accidentally used coins, but not me! I figured since I had taken the money out of their jar, the prize belonged to them, and I gave them the whole jackpot.

When I was older and remembered this, the memory shocked me, and I suddenly realized that no matter how much money tried to flow to me, I kept pushing it away. I couldn't receive or grow money because loyalty to my family system's "honor and integrity OR money" program wouldn't let me. Because I could only see money as bad and wrong, or else as something I should work hard for, it couldn't have a kind and gentle place in my life, and it certainly couldn't be a friend.

This realization inspired my first "money walk and talk."

I was tired and discouraged by my negative relationship with money (and how little I had in my life). I looked at the world around me, and there seemed to be really kind people who had a lot of money and who did good things with it. I realized that I wanted to do that too. So, I decided to go for a walk and have a conversation with money. Yes, a literal conversation.

"Good morning, Money," I ventured, rather formally. "I've been aware of you most of my life, but I don't think I know you well enough to form a relationship with you. I'd really like to have more of you around in my world. So, it seems important to get to know you."

The next words out of my mouth and the accompanying emotions surprised the heck out of me. "I think I have known you and loved who you really are since I was small!" As I spoke these surprising words, I felt a shift, and it triggered a flood of tears, insights, and memories, starting with my memory of collecting canna seeds in order to create a garden of beauty. And can you believe it? I picked up a $10 bill, a $20 bill, and a $100 bill walking home that day! All three at different places, just waiting for me to notice them! On the way back from that walk, $130 dollars richer, a simple sentence kept popping up over and over again. "Look at the work you do. It's all right there."

Of course, it was! My systemic language and inherited money DNA were keeping me in a state of separation from money, abundance, and flow. I would have to form an entirely different relationship with it and create the shift I was teaching.

It was the first of many conversations money and I would have over the years. Having had so little money for such a long time, and having constructed some well-defined fears and limitations around it, I was eager to resume the adventure I had begun as a child, before all the dos and don'ts had crept in. I promised myself that I would look at money with kind and happy eyes. That I would explore the ways it could flow with generosity and joy, and that I would give it a place in my heart and teach others how it was a good friend.

The journey to changing my money DNA began with me putting down my resistance and unconscious loyalties, bit by bit, and being willing to look in places that felt a little scary at first. I had to move beyond the dos and don'ts in my system into what was possible. That process began with three things: (1) One new thought: "Is there a different side to money that I don't know?" (2) One new feeling: a tickle of possibility and a subtle sense in my stomach of allowing and imagining. (3) One new action: consistent conversations with the universe and money that pushed me beyond my comfort zone.

Eventually I learned not to give my services and time away. I learned to say, "Yes," when offered good compensation for what I was doing. I paid attention to the balance of give and receive in my life. It also meant making sure that whatever I was offering was of good and fair value and that I was *not* over-giving all the time.

As a child and young adult, I'd unconsciously found a way to have a relationship with money that had locked me into a particular bandwidth, and I had to learn to move beyond that.

I couldn't stay unconscious if I wished to change.

Systemic Steppingstone #22:
Money Questions

Here are some of the questions I asked myself as I began to learn about and teach money DNA. Start asking yourself questions like these. You will be surprised by some of the answers! They gave me insight, momentum, ideas, and direction.

1. When did I first become aware of money?

2. How was money seen in my family, culture, and country?

3. Whose viewpoint of money impacted me the most? What did they say, and was the impact scary or inspiring?

4. What judgments do I hold about people who have a lot of money? What do I think of them? What words do I use to describe them?

5. What judgments do I hold about people who don't have money? What do I think of them? What words do I use to describe them?

6. What judgments do I hold about myself in relation to money?

7. What is my biggest fear around money?

8. Am I the only one with that kind of fear? Or did I inherit it from someone in my family system?

9. How would I like these judgments and fears to shift?

10. How might my life change if they did?

11. What one new thought, feeling, and action could I have around money that I could really embody?

MONEY AND THE SYSTEMIC PRINCIPLES

Looking at money DNA through the lens of the systemic principles of belonging, order, and the balance of give and receive, you can quickly identify which one has you stuck and home in on all the nuances of *how* you are stuck. Then you can begin to shift, because remember: the truth is what you make it.

Money DNA and Belonging

Family, organizational, religious, cultural, and national systems have written and unwritten rules around money and belonging. They often take the form of common knowledge sentences, moral codes, stories, warnings, and expectations. These rules are designed to show you how to *be* in order to *belong* within those systems. Some are empowering, some are limiting, and all are powerful. The ways you align with them shape how much money you will or won't, can or can't, make, have, keep, or lose.

These rules and your unconscious loyalties to them create a money bandwidth within which you operate, and you feel it keenly when you exceed or drop below it. I often see clients who cannot attain a certain income because "it would be an *obscene* amount of money." Notice the systemic word and the immediate judgment that locks these clients into a tight money bandwidth?

Financial systemic sentences and actions as the result of events spawn entire generations of dos and don'ts, cans and can'ts that create a sense of belonging when you adhere to them and a sense of separation from your system when you don't.

Sentences that show up around *belonging* and money include:

- It's not nice to talk about money.
- It's not about the money.
- Only greedy people have money.
- We don't need much.
- Love is more important than money.
- A fool and his money are soon parted.
- A penny saved is a penny earned.
- A good name is better than riches.

With sentences like these running rampant in your mind every time you come into contact with money, how is it possible to have a money attitude of thriving? You may also take on limiting actions that are unique to you and your system financially, repeating money patterns that may have been passed down through the generations, such as:

- Not looking at your finances
- Running up credit card debt
- Spending it all as soon you receive it
- Hoarding it
- Making money and giving it away, and not being able to enjoy it

Find out how you much you align with your family's money DNA in limiting ways. Go back and look at your responses to Systemic Steppingstone #22 and see what patterns you notice. Ask what started the patterns and whose thoughts, feelings, or actions you may be replicating. Always ask, "What could I do with more?" This question stimulates your wants, gives money a place to flow, and fosters evolution. Don't try to figure out how to get money. Figure out how to get your foot off the brake, open the window, and let it flow in.

Money DNA and Order

Order creates its own set of money DNA patterns and can influence the flow of money in your life. Position in the family may mean that as eldest, you inherit the most. In some families and cultures, gender plays a role in who carries the most weight or influence, and money DNA is created around that. Do you find your money DNA driven by any of the following influences?

- The inheritance goes to the eldest.
- Men get the money, and women marry well for their financial safety.
- Men are the providers and carry the family name.

In organizations, compensation is often related to skill set, time in the company, and also gender. This too creates money DNA through systemic sentences and actions, patterns, and loyalties to those patterns. Is your money DNA driven by any of the following?

Skill set
- White- and blue-collar jobs
- The top brains get the most money
- Experts get paid the most
- Bonuses for brains
- C-suite, middle management, entry level

Time in company
- Golden handcuffs
- Golden handshake
- Bonuses for longevity

Gender

- Women choose to have children and take time off
- Strong male leaders, difficult female leaders

I know it may seem like *all* of the above are in operation, but usually one of the three categories is dominant and will become obvious once you begin looking at all the sayings, beliefs, and actions in your own systems. Once you understand which of the three principles are financially supportive for you and which are problematic, it's time to look a little deeper at the nuances and particulars of what may be creating limitations.

Money DNA and the Balance of Give and Receive

Depending on our sense of self and our credibility in our social and family systems with regards to money, we tend to sense quite quickly when we are being over- or under-compensated. However, if we were brought up to be overly good mannered or to "not be greedy," we may numb that inherent compass and settle for less to be in harmony with the system. *The rules of the system trump personal reality.*

For individuals with an imbalance of give and receive in their money DNA, you might hear things like:

- I don't need to be paid. I just do it for the love of it.
- Recognition is all I need.
- I don't need much to get by.
- I don't have all the degrees behind my name,
  so I can't earn more.
- It's much easier for me to give than to receive.
- This is sacred work, and I can't charge for it.

Someone with a balance of give and receive knows how much to give and what their value is, and works to improve that value. They treat their careers as though they were their children, nurturing and growing them so that they, too, can evolve their financial worth.

You don't have to be a big lawyer or CEO to develop a solid financial presence. I travel all over the world to deliver events and train other facilitators, and I pay attention to elevated attitude. Waiting tables and driving taxis, to name just two, are careers where I have seen some people make a lot of money and some not so much. The top earners tap into and grow healthy attitudes about themselves, others, and money, knowing that *who* they are and how they feel and radiate, not *what* they do, brings them the money they want. They go over and above. People want to be around them because they value their customers, and customers like to reward good service.

In organizations you can tell quite quickly if the organization compensates fairly or if there is an imbalance of give and receive. You may hear negative sentences like these.

- We are on the clock 24/7.
- They keep expecting us to do more and more for less and less.
- We are told we should just be grateful we have a job.
- We have been given impossible targets yet again.
- We are expected to put in as much time as the founders yet receive little in return.

Some positive sentences you might hear:

- I work hard, but the compensation is great.
- I always feel valued and validated.
- The incentives keep me engaged and motivated.
- The personal and professional growth opportunities are great here.

People pay more for good service. They also equate what is charged with your level of expertise. If you overcharge people, they will know it, *but* the same applies when you undercharge. People may assume you are not as good as you might be. As a species we often equate our safety with expertise and price point. We all want to "be in good hands!"

THE SEVEN LEVELS OF MONEY DNA

Your current financial circumstances are *not* a reflection of your future once you start changing your money DNA. Changing your thoughts and feelings can change your life. Do it consciously and you turbocharge that change. Money is no different from any other force. It's the *way* you focus on it that creates your relationship with it.

Check out the image below. My systemic explanation of the levels will provide you with a quick way to identify where you may be with your own money DNA.

7 Levels of Money Through a Systemic Lens

Flow

Level	Unhealthy Motivations	Taking responsibility; in service to larger systems and people	Healthy Motivations
7	N/A	Service	I am abundance itself and infinite flow.
6	N/A	Impact	I am abundant. I enjoy and respect money and am a wise steward. I fund a better world.
5	N/A	Coherence	I've made it. How can I grow money with others? My dreams are coming true.
4	N/A	Transformation	Limitation doesn't serve me or the system. I can have as much as I want.
3	I am not worthy of wealth. I haven't done enough to earn it. I give it away.	Self-Esteem	I work hard for what I have. I have money. I have worth.
2	My parents/system didn't have money. I won't either. I am not allowed.	Relationship	I have enough money. I am allowed to belong.
1	I'll never have enough money. You can't get rich ethically.	Survival	I will do what it takes to ethically take care of my financial needs.

Blocked
Blind loyalty to family system

Levels 1-3: Blind, Reactive, Closed, Survival-Based Money DNA

In these levels, money DNA is rooted in survival and struggle. But, as you can see from the chart above, our language and actions can be healthy and encouraging or unhealthy and limiting. Here are some of the typical money dynamics found at these levels.

- We constantly work at being "okay" and having "enough" and try to appear like we have our lives together.

- We experience varying states of worry and discomfort.

- Money seems materialistic, threatening, and precarious.

- We judge ourselves and others for having or not having money.

- Thought cycles tend to focus on struggle, overwhelm, survival, searches for temporary relief, and fear-based drive.

- Feelings can vary from short-lived gratification and relaxation to sadness, fear, and lack of self-worth, drive, and determination.

- Actions can range from building self-worth and expertise to spending blindly, hoarding, and self-exclusion.

Level 4: Money DNA Becomes Transformational

At this level we begin to realize that our limited programs around money don't serve us or the larger system. It occurs to us that our thoughts, feelings, and actions may be driving some of our results. We realize there are other possibilities and begin to take responsibility.

- We begin to challenge some of the thoughts and feelings we hold about money.

- We look at those who have it and understand that they are doing something different. Instead of judging, we become curious. How are they doing it?

- There is excitement as we realize a better relationship with money is possible, is allowed, and could create some incredible changes for us.

Levels 5 & Up: Successful, Open-Hearted, Creative

At this point, money DNA shifts us from struggle to flow, from materialistic to spiritual and heart-centered. We are rewriting the limiting money patterns in our system, changing our financial destiny, and we begin to use positive sentences of re-solution.

- My relationship with money is joyful, fun, and filled with gratitude.

- Money is a spiritual force and flow in my life.

- I am free of limiting thoughts and actions around money. I enjoy and love it.

- I acknowledge that I have money and am successful. I demonstrate what's possible and show others how to get there too.

- I am grateful. I give thanks for money every day and it flows.

- I am a wise steward of this flow. I respect it and learn its language.

- I know that money is energy, just like love.

- I help fund a better, kinder world.

- I radiate abundance.

- I am abundance.

CREATING HEALTHY MONEY DNA

You've already contemplated events in your family system that affected the financial status of its members. You've also examined what your country, ethnicity, and culture say about money and answered the money questions in Steppingstone #22. And you've determined which systemic principle—belonging, order, or balance of give and receive—most drives your current relationship with money. Now it's time to dig deeper. Ask yourself:

- What negative words and phrases do I use around money?

- What negative actions do I take?

- What are my fears and excuses around wanting money and committing to having it?

212

- Do I feel guilty when I am doing well financially?
- In what ways do I sabotage my money health? Do I waste it? Lose it? Ignore it?

Now you have your hidden saboteurs lined up. Thank them and use them as a source of wisdom and warning. These are the pieces you want to let go or move *from*. Now, let's look at how you build healthy money DNA.

- Develop respect for money and how it supports your life in a healthy way.
- Create positive language, thoughts, and feelings around it. Mindfully reframe any limiting thoughts, feelings, and actions around it.
- Be open to *all* the ways money can come to you.
- Pay attention to how you are using and gaining value from it.
- Ask yourself how you can be a good friend to money.

And then . . . drumroll please! Have at least two conversations with money!

Systemic Steppingstone #23:
Talking with Money

Most of my clients think I've lost it when I ask them to have a series of talks with money. But doing the unusual is what starts to move things, and they soon find out that it works and end up enjoying it. Part of the reason it works is that it's a way to bring your subconscious money issues and patterns to the fore, enabling you to focus on changing the patterns that don't serve you, shifting those well-installed neural pathways, and moving *to* what you want.

CONVERSATION #1:
YOUR *FROM* CONVERSATION

Your first conversation should be about what's familiar for you, namely your issues and struggles with money, your multigenerational system's dialogue around it, and so forth. It will help if you use a representative for money (a dollar bill or some denomination). Place it on the floor or on the table in front of you where you can see it and talk to it. Take your time and be as honest and open as you can.

Please share with money:

- What you think, feel, and do around it

- What you say about it

- What your parents and others taught you about it

- Your biggest fear or sadness around it

- Why and how you push it away

- Why you believe you don't deserve to have it or be in a good relationship with it

- One thing you really want to tell money but don't dare

- One thought, feeling, or action you would like to change around it

This conversation will show you what you have made money mean in your life and how you have made that your truth.

CONVERSATION #2:
YOUR *TO* CONVERSATION

This conversation is about changing your relationship with money and creating your new future with it. Only have this conversation when you are really willing to talk, listen, and shift. (*Shift* means letting go of excuses and resistance

and being open to doing something entirely different.)
Remember, money is flow and a meta-force (one of the
global life forces that affect humanity on a large scale).
It can and does respond to the ways you interact with it.
Here are the things I want you to share with money:

- What do you like most about money?

- How do you feel when it is present in your life?

- What do you most like to *do* with it?

- How is money a friend to you?

- For what do you owe it thanks?

Once you get your answers, it's time to contemplate
the following:

- What does your ideal relationship with money look
  like?

- How do you move toward that?

- What pattern with money is trying to emerge through
  you?

- What is your ideal systemic money sentence?

- What one shift in your thoughts, feelings, language, or
  actions would facilitate that new pattern?

- How might you be a wise steward of money in your
  world?

- Who will benefit from your stewardship?

During these conversations, remember to open your
eyes, heart, mind, and gut and consciously create your new
money DNA with kindness, inclusion, enjoyment, and
gratitude. That keeps you safe and in good standing with
your higher self, allowing you to create fearlessly.

Switch money languages. *Suffering* is one financial
language. *Contributing, thriving, and playing* is another.

Look for your hidden loyalties and reframe them into towering strengths. Walk away from discouragement or use it to create resolve. Focus on what you want, not what you don't have. Moving toward something ignites hope. Moving away from something can cause struggle and effort. *Always* celebrate your wins. View multigenerational events and family feedback that might cause setbacks or limitations with kind eyes. Remember, they ignited your desire for something different. Explore the surfacing patterns and choose what to lay down, what to continue, and where to create something new. Dare to take steps beyond the current limiting rules of your system.

Creating successful money DNA is as much a part of healthy, happy living as exercising your body and your mind. Just like your physical and mental health, it requires commitment and the formation of strong, positive habits to support your path.

Each individual's destiny with money is quite different. When you desire greatly and want a lot of money in your life, and you dare to achieve what you desire, you are changing your world and the community around you. Changing your money DNA isn't difficult or tedious unless you tell yourself that it is. Sure, it's easy to fall off the wagon. We all do from time to time. If you do, don't be discouraged. Buy another ticket and get back on! The choice for financial freedom or financial bondage is yours. Whichever path you forge more consistently will determine your money DNA lens and the ways in which you can or cannot use money to create a better world for you and those around you. If you view money as a friend and create an adventure with it, that's how it will show up for you.

CHAPTER 16

COMMUNIQUÉS
FROM THE BODY

Health DNA

In systemic work and constellations, we constantly see how the body does its best to bring unconscious personal and systemic patterns to the forefront of our attention so they can be swiftly dealt with. Everything in our lives is geared to bring imbalance to our awareness so it can be corrected. Our language, our choices, our emotional suffering, and our physical issues are all there to drive us inward on a path of personal discovery so we might apply our uniquely human ability to choose something different and begin the process of creating new patterns of emotional DNA, which helps us to change our lives for the better.

A no-nonsense, blunt translator, the body's ups and downs are often a good guide to whether you are on or off track, providing an exquisite compass for where you are and where you want to be. Your body also reacts to generational patterns. Your nervous system is not just *your* nervous system; many of its patterns, blocks, and triggers are multigenerational. Some of your health responses may come from years of conditioning, abuse, lack of self-worth, social indoctrination, and so forth. But sometimes illnesses show up that may have arisen generations ago, expressing through you every time the generational trigger is activated. With insight and willingness, intention and work, these physical conditions can be changed and the trigger transformed into a launch pad.

Let me tell you a personal story.

Several years ago, I was traveling, talking, and teaching nonstop. I had a rapidly growing list of clients, and making sure that everyone's needs were well met and that I got everything "right" every moment of every day consumed my life. Systemic work and constellations were important, leading-edge stuff and very new, and I was all too aware that if it wasn't presented properly, its enormous potential for helping people wouldn't actualize.

I worked and worked and didn't pay attention to my body's need for rest and nutrition. I started taking over-the-counter pain relievers for headaches induced by long hours hunched over documents and presentations—and I didn't pay attention to the fact that you shouldn't take them on an empty stomach. I was too busy to eat. I was also overwhelmed by the increasing number of systemic sentences populating my thoughts:

- You don't know what you're doing.

- You have to get this right or they won't want you anymore.

- This is so new, nobody will listen unless you present it perfectly.

- If it's worth doing, it's worth doing well.

- Give people as much value as you possibly can.

- Don't take your eye off the ball for an instant or you will lose it all.

- This hasn't been done before. What makes you think you can do it?

- Make sure you don't freeze or go off track.

- You don't ever quit!

It was like *Monsters, Inc.* in my brain, and I soon paid the price. Flying from my Texas home through London to South Africa to teach a class, I became horribly ill. My stomach hurt, and I kept fading in and out of consciousness. I couldn't eat or drink because it sent my stomach into knots of pain and nausea. I knew I was in trouble, but I had work to do! They'd flown me in, and I was going to deliver no matter what. Every night after class, I would shake going to bed and pretty much pass out rather than sleep. It got so bad that I wound up teaching from bed the final day.

I have never been so sick or so scared. When I got back to the States, my physician suspected a severe stomach ulcer and wanted some tests done, and I said no. I had a high workload and didn't have the time. And I really didn't want to deal with all sorts of medical rounds and tests. Instead, I asked for a month to see if I could turn it around myself and got serious.

I went looking for those systemic sentences about my work and the fears I had around it. I wrote them down and then explored their origins—which turned out to be quite obvious. In my family, you don't quit, you always deliver, and you deliver quality that's more than worth its price. You take care of family, and you make sure they are safe no matter what.

My grandfather on my mother's side had had stomach ulcers from stress when jobs were scarce and the family was in trouble. As a young man, my father's family had almost gone under when his father walked away and left. There was a lot of stress around survival, and my father had stomach issues that were partially a result of having typhoid as a kid and partially a result of stress from taking care of everyone. Later, as a new father, my dad stepped up to take care of the family and had a heart attack at an incredibly young age. He worked long hours, and his premature demise was partially due to the stress of moving to the US and watching a business opportunity get snatched away. He was terrified that he'd made a wrong decision that had put the family in danger. After my father died, it was clear it was up to me to make sure the family was safe.

So, there it was. The poison in my brain and body was stress from the fear of not being able to take care of my family. When I was stressed, my unconscious loyalty to my father and grandfather targeted my stomach, just like their stress had. I had also had a teacher who told me I would never be able to write well and, of course, teachers are always right! No wonder one of my biggest stressors was creating course material and workbooks. No wonder I wouldn't believe it when people told me how good my course content was. No wonder every time I had to create new material, I wanted to throw the cats out one window and my computer out the other.

Realizing all this, I started to laugh. I am good at helping people work through their own imposter syndrome, and here I was, bang in the middle of my own. I needed these deadly systemic patterns to grow into something else through me.

So, what was the antidote?

- I *forced* myself to accept the positive feedback I was getting from corporations and individuals. People kept coming back for more because they were transforming, and either everyone else was collectively stupid or I was delivering something useful. Accepting reality was a point of relaxation for me.

- As I relaxed, I began to realize that I really enjoyed what I was doing, and *that* allowed me more breathing room and even more relaxation.

- I took all my systemic sentences and created sentences of re-solution:

  - *You have to get this right or they won't want you anymore* became *You are delivering something useful. Just keep growing and enjoy it.*

  - *This is so new, who will listen?* turned into *Neuroscience and epigenetics are good allies, and people are listening and experiencing change.*

  - *Make sure you don't freeze or go off track* was now *I love what I am talking about. When I tune in, I can talk about this for hours.*

  - *This hasn't been done before, so why do you think you can do it?* became *Someone's got to do it, so I guess that will be me!* (I *loved* that one. It was a direct link to what I'd promised about making magic at age nine. That one sunk in all the way to my bones.)

  - *You don't quit* turned into *Take a small break and smell the roses.* (This one allows me to exhale and do what I love to do the most—play!)

  - *You don't know what you're doing* was so ridiculous I couldn't even hold onto it anymore.

When I looked at my body, I had to ask myself, "What can you not stomach?" And the answer was, "Failing to look after my family." So, who did *that* belong to? My father. My mother's father. My father's father who walked away from his family. I had those three ancestors to thank for my relentless drive to create safety. But now it was time to relax, enjoy, and work from a space of balance and love rather than fear in ways *they* had not been able to do. Today, I am often told that people attend my events and classes because they feel safe there, and feeling safe enables them to explore their lives and transform them. When safety stopped being fear-based and transformed into a drive to create stability and joy for my family, it was a huge relief. It unleashed an excitement to see what I could achieve. And my gut relaxed and transformed from a repository of old fears into an inner compass.

Once I identified the limiting thoughts and feelings, I set about reframing each one of them. That was key. Not only did I focus on changing in the moment, but I also worked on changing in the future. I imagined myself teaching at events, feeling loving, relaxed, and playful as I watched others shift. I imagined it so clearly that I felt and experienced myself in the future. By the time I got around to having the medical tests done, all was well with my stomach. "You had a lucky escape," my doctor said.

I didn't. I took the time to engage in a much-needed mindful reconnaissance and re-creation. I experienced firsthand the power of systemic work and constellations.

THE BODY KNOWS

Meditation and mindfulness practices are wonderful for getting the body to relax in general. But when we face dysfunction and illness, it's not so easy to get the body to respond the way we wish. Have you ever tried telling your body to just get over a headache or a muscle spasm?

Tell your body to heal without addressing the root cause and watch it refuse. It knows that something is off, and it's not about to let you forget either. A stomachache is an obvious prompt to ask what (or who) is happening in your life that you can't stomach anymore. A kidney or bladder infection is a pretty straightforward message directing your attention to what has you so pissed off. Stiffness and joint issues point toward inflexibility and stubbornness. The book *Heal Your Body: The Mental Causes for Physical Illness and the Metaphysical Way to Overcome Them* by Louise Hay is a tremendous source of insights into the body's many messages. The sooner you listen and uncover the root cause, the quicker your body can respond and heal. Being willing, aware, and proactive is the key to healing and change.

In Nick's family, everyone was terrified of heart disease. His great-great-grandfather had heart disease and refused to see a doctor about it. After he lost his business, he lost his purpose in life, hardly ate, and dropped dead of a heart attack at age forty-five. Great-grandfather never got over that. He, too, developed heart disease and keeled over at the age of forty-six. Nick's grandfather had heart disease and died of heart failure at forty-seven. His father took a little better care of himself, ate a little better, and tried to manage his stress. He died at fifty-three.

Notice how the unconscious loyalties created a line of inevitability for all the men in the family. Also notice that each subsequent generation of men lived just a little longer than their predecessor. They were gradually stair-stepping their way out of the pattern, but because family members were taught to see heart disease as an inevitable hereditary thing rather than a pattern that was theirs to change ("Heart disease runs in our family and kills the men"), there was no real way to break the pattern. Then came Nick.

Aware of the pattern and his opportunity to live his life differently, Nick determined, "I am *not* going to meet the same fate as my ancestors. I want to see my children grow up and have children of their own. Something has to change here, and it starts with me."

As a young man Nick made sure to follow a heart healthy diet and exercise daily. He saw his doctor regularly and took supplements. He educated himself about cardiopulmonary disease and all the things he could do to have a different outcome, including meditating regularly and visualizing his healthy heart. Now in his sixties, Nick has broken the epigenetic pattern. His children are aware of the family predisposition, but rather than being frightened by it, they use it as a good reason to create a healthy lifestyle. The multigenerational nervous system is moving from fear-based survival to purpose-based, healthy thriving.

Systemic Steppingstone #24:
Tracking Your Health Systemically

Although medical intervention is important and physical and mental health conditions require professional attention beyond the work we do here, to create a difference in your health, you want to look at your current health and its roots. Does your family system reflect health or illness? Which of the two patterns is more common in your system? Which has the stronger family pull, and how does that affect the family system itself? Is there a pattern of suffering or a deep desire to thrive?

Are there chronic illnesses or conditions in the family? When did they start? What was happening at the time? How did this affect you and others in your system? Ask yourself, "When did this start for me? What was happening in my life at the time? How did/does it affect me? What do I say about this? What words do I use to describe this illness? What choices do I make? What does it allow me to do/stop me from doing?"

If you are struggling with a health condition, take a moment to write the condition down on a piece of paper and place it on the floor in front of you.

- Walk toward it and notice your thoughts, feelings, and actions around it.

- What does this stop you from doing?

- What does it enable you to do?

- Did this pattern begin with you or with someone else in the family?

- How does this condition allow you to belong in or exclude you from the family system?

- What would you like to say to it?

To heal your body, it's important to understand the hints, clues, origins, and makeup of what it is expressing. The examples in the next sections will give you an idea of the systemic approach to exploring and resolving health issues. Please be aware that this is *not* medical advice but educational and systemic information that can prove useful on your own conscious journey to wellness.

DRUG ADDICTION

Systemically, addiction is generally seen as a matter of belonging, or more accurately, exclusion. People who carry the addiction pattern in a family system can also carry a pattern of victim-perpetrator where neither side has been identified or given a place to belong. In the case of the latter, both sides express in one body: "I, the perpetrator, hurt myself, the victim."

You might want to look for such a pattern in your own life or in someone in your family system. The solution is to give each a place in your heart and not carry them in your body. You are restoring their place and their belonging. The burden is not yours to carry. You have seen what no one else will look at. Now, it's time to move forward.

ALCOHOLISM

This condition is often seen systemically as a way to die to what is in front of you—a way to not look or to remove oneself from the horror of an event not processed. It is a slow suicide, and the question must be asked, "What is so bad that you cannot look?" We might also ask, "Who do you wish to follow into absenteeism and death?"

Alcoholism is known to travel through multiple generations, and often its origins are contained in a large event that could not or would not be looked at. This creates an unconscious loyalty that echoes through the generations. The solution here is to realize that you cannot carry the burden of another, or if it is your own burden, that it serves no one and nothing.

Let others, as well as the burden itself, know that you will use it to create something stronger and happier, acknowledging the original creator of the pattern. For example, if your culture was destroyed, instead of walking the path of sorrow and suppression, commit to being the joy and success that newly defines your culture through you. If this happened directly to you, give thanks for a new day and commit to developing thoughts and feelings that are stronger than the ones that hold you prisoner right now. You are strong enough to have developed the first set of thoughts and feelings, which means you are strong enough to put a healthy set of thoughts and feelings into play as well.

When you use alcohol to numb out or quiet an overactive nervous system, alcohol can feel like a friend and comforter for a while. But eventually you are going to need to process what got you there, piece by careful piece. This is a systemic journey best taken with a very good systemic guide who can help you to see your limits and walk you through them very slowly, so you disentangle and then build a healthy mind and body, one word, phrase, and feeling at a time.

ARTHRITIS

Arthritis often walks into the room as either anger or guilt. It's not always the client's condition but sometimes inherited. The minute I hear, "Arthritis runs in our family," I go looking for who or what created the pattern and how it is echoing through the system. Whether it is guilt or anger, there tends to be a stiffening of the joints, a rigidity, and a tightly held emotion that is not being expressed or processed. Sometimes the event is not spoken of for fear of inflaming the situation, and then the inflammation presents internally. Sometimes this is an issue around belonging, and both the event and the excluded issue need to be processed and given a place to belong in a way that reduces inflammation.

BACKACHE

Backache and neck ache can occur when we unconsciously refuse to acknowledge those who came before us and/or reject them outright. We stiffen, refusing to be small and bow gently to the flow of life, love, and fulfillment. This can occur as the result of an experience that is a jolt to the system, triggering distrust in the parents. Perhaps they tell the children that boys will inherit the estate and girls won't, they spent the money that was in your college fund, or they have affairs and you get caught in the middle of them.

Being out of order and being above the parents, having to become the parent, or looking down on them can also create an inflexibility that translates to pain in the neck and back. This can also happen when as a child you have to take on a burden that is too big for you, causing stress to your back and neck. The solution here is to look carefully at the burden and see how it has served you, and also to see what part of that burden you can put down.

Jill had had a backache for years. She'd tried everything medical and was ready to do something different, so she came to an event. We set up a constellation, placing representatives for her mom, her dad, and the backache. I asked her to take her own place in the constellation rather than use a representative. She did so with hands clenched tightly, and she backed away from her parents. When I asked what had happened, she replied, "They completely disrespected the way I was raising my kids. So, I don't let them see them anymore."

In systemic work we sometimes ask participants to bow to those who came before them as a sign of acknowledgment of their place and to show who belongs where in the order of things. I asked Jill if she might be able to bow to her parents who came before her, and her back stiffened. She clenched her teeth and shook her head. I asked her what she liked about her parents and the ways she had been raised. As she spoke about their family dynamics, she stiffened and relaxed in response to what she had and hadn't liked. Eventually, she grudgingly acknowledged that she had turned out okay, and that up until her parents had given their grandchildren some candy—which Jill didn't allow—family visits had been pleasant . . . and her back hadn't hurt.

"So, what did they do as grandparents that was okay and fun?" I asked.

"They really knew how to celebrate the holidays," she said, smiling reminiscently.

"Can you bow to that?" I asked. She did with somewhat of a grin. "What else can you bow to and thank them for?"

Before she could answer, a look of astonishment crossed her face. "Oh, my God! My backache's gone!" she cried.

Just that small bow—that act of honest recognition and honoring—shifted everything for Jill. As we explored further, it wasn't lost on her that it was something sweet that had triggered her falling out with her parents. She commented that she had always thought her grandmother was too harsh. Within a few minutes, she had recognized that her own reaction to the candy incident and her resulting rigidity were repeats of her grandmother's inflexibility and lack of sweetness. Once Jill could see the pattern, she could set it down and realize that sometimes a little sweetness in life is allowed. Her backache never returned, and her parents and children see each other often.

DEPRESSION

Depression shows up as a lack of energy, a block in the flow of energy, or an inability to receive the flow of energy from one generation to the next. It shows up as lack of fulfillment, an inability to accept things that have happened—connections not made, love not given, worthiness not felt, substance not gained. It is accompanied by an unkind, self-defeating, punishing sense of inevitability and futility. Something went wrong, and it's all over. A decision has been made personally or somewhere in the system that seems undoable and inescapable.

Systemic work is helpful here, especially using constellations as a way to finally be able to see and experience what has happened, hear the language that is keeping you stuck, and begin to see, speak, and feel your way out of what feels like a mess and into the flow of life again.

Depression can also be seen as the end to an old pattern, signaling the deep need for a new one. If depression lives in you, you may be both the concluder and the beginner. This is something you might explore with a systemic worker, therapist, or someone who is skilled at walking you through this. The principle involved might be any one of the three depending on the event, but the process and outcome are to give the old pattern its place after resolving what wants to stop, and then to give the new pattern its place in your heart as you move forward.

DIABETES

Some forms of diabetes stem from an inability to generate, process, or take in the sweetness of life. This condition often runs in families, and systemically we ask, "Where did this begin? How did it affect the original member of the system? How is it affecting subsequent members? What wants to stop, and what wants to start in order to change this?" This condition is, like most others, highly unique to the precipitating event and the choices and decisions made. The resolution is tailored accordingly.

HYPOCHONDRIA

People who have been told they have hypochondria often haven't been given the answers they need in order to know that they and their bodies are okay. Something has been said, not said, or not addressed in the area of the body's health, and unconsciously it preys upon the person's mind, placing them in what seems to be an inescapable limbo and an ongoing quest for the information or words that will allow the body to know that it is well.

Hypochondria can also express when an illness or condition was excluded or unaddressed in a prior generation. Once it is seen and acknowledged, the client can finally put down the systemic ghost they have been carrying in their minds and bodies and move on. The body is smart. It holds onto what you can't or won't process until you do.

INFERTILITY

Infertility is one of the most interesting spaces to explore systemically. In brief, we often see that a woman or her line or a man or his line do not feel safe to create and pass on life. This can happen as a result of rape, where the act of producing life is unconsciously associated with invasion, shock, damage, and the threat of death. I have seen it where there was a rapist in the man's line and subsequent members were infertile. It also appears when having children was not a happy event, or being a child in an unhappy family shut down the desire for a family that might repeat the pattern. Guilt, anger, and withholding are also patterning that I have seen around infertility.

In each case, we traced back to the event that started it all, then created new language, feelings, and actions that made creating life possible, devoid of shame, danger, or burden. Even in cases where discovering the initial event is not possible, creating new language, feelings, and actions around conception or raising a family often changes the situation.

OBESITY

In systemic work, when clients are obese and cannot lose weight, it's helpful to ask when they began to notice that they were putting on weight and what was happening in their lives at that time. Sometimes we notice that a traumatic event creates a need to protect one's body from being abused or invaded, and the client may do this unconsciously by taking on weight as a protective mechanism. It's important to notice that often the threat has come and gone, but the client is still holding onto the weight as though the event were happening right now. In some ways, it still is, since they haven't been able to shift their words, thoughts, and feelings beyond what happened. Completion needs to occur. The event needs to be given a place in the system and then new words, thoughts, sentences of re-solution, and feelings created and lived.

Sometimes we notice that clients unconsciously expand their mass to include members of the family system who are missing or excluded. They sense an important lack or absence in their system and try to fill it by including the weight of the one who is not there.

Lack of love and nurturing are also a common factor. Humans are meant to receive and consume large amounts of emotional food and nurturing and moderate amounts of physical food. When we don't receive the emotional food we need, our brains can become confused. What we can't take in through our hearts, we try to take in through our mouths. Emotional and physical food are out of order, and we start to take in more physical food than we should to make up for the lack of emotional nutrition. Once you look at what's missing and find the needed emotional food, the physical food can take its rightful place again.

The body can be quite literal. I have had clients who tell me that when they need nurturing, they look for something sticky and sweet—in other words, mother's milk!

Systemic Steppingstone #25:
The Happily Inevitable Path
to a Healthier Life

Teaching ourselves good health means teaching ourselves self-love and self-care, and the first step to self-love is being open to seeing what you want from life rather than feeling like life is happening to you. You have to be willing to take responsibility for growing your life consciously. Once you move into the place of self-responsibility and start taking steps to shift old patterns of thought and action, your brain can move from a place of reactivity to creativity in all areas of your life, including your health.

- Remember the three principles—belonging, order, and balance of give and receive. Look at which of the three your challenge sorts into. See if anything needs to be completed, flipped, or reframed using the condition and principle as your guide.

- Listen to your body and learn to translate symptoms into messages. For example, if you experience stomach pains, what can you not stomach? If you're anxious all the time, what have you not resolved that leaves you frightened? If you're overweight, who or what are you holding onto? What are you guarding yourself against? If you have hearing problems, what is difficult to hear?

- Learn to listen and be open to receive. Where are you at odds with yourself? What do you need to say "yes" to? To whom or what do you need to say "no?" Is peace trying to emerge? Feel where peace resides in your body and let it expand.

Sometimes the illness is the cure. I once had a client who was proud of the fact that he didn't take a single penny from his parents. He didn't need them for anything—until he became ill and needed their love and support. Bridging the divide that had been there for years, finally, he could receive from his parents. That single act turned his life around. Once things were back in order, love could flow again, and he flourished.

Remember, the body doesn't lie. Symptoms, no matter how painful, are there as guideposts to help you on your way.

CHAPTER 17

SYSTEMIC WORK AND CONSTELLATIONS IN SERVICE OF GLOBAL TRANSFORMATION

I am often asked where I think systemic work and constellations could be most effective and what my long-term vision for this work is. The quick answer is that it's effective for people everywhere, in every walk of life, as a path to transformation and expansion beyond past limitations and ancient history. My vision for this work is vast numbers of people exploring their multigenerational history and patterns in order to fully reveal their own destiny and step into the creation of their best selves. The world can't help but become a better place when our best selves show up!

If we use this work wisely and fully, we stand a strong chance of evolving to a place humanity hasn't reached before, where the game to be played is bigger and more rewarding.

People also ask me if this is spiritual work. I can only say that if you're reaching beyond who you think you are and into the world of possibility, growing into the highest version of yourself and discovering the sacredness of life and how we are all ultimately connected as one, how could it be anything else?

The first time I participated in a constellation, I had no idea what I was in for. I'd been invited to attend and was chosen to represent a member of a client's family. For the first few minutes, I wondered if I was supposed to do or say something, and then I remembered that we'd been instructed to simply let the system flow through us and respond only if compelled "by the field." It sounded a little out there, but I was there to learn something new and stay open.

Suddenly my body whipped around, and I found myself backing away from another "member of the family" filled with a deep sense of anger. I knew the anger wasn't mine. All the same, it was flaring within me like a rocket on the Fourth of July!

What followed I can only describe as a deep and profound dance between the client's system and each one of us representatives. My sense of time fell away, and so did my sense of the rest of the room as I responded to other members within the system. When I was asked what I was feeling and if there was anything I needed to say, what came out of my mouth had nothing to do with the everyday me. I was in service to the client's system, responding to and with its language. The client gained insights, shifted profoundly, and was visibly changed.

I was floored. My body, mind, and spirit had never been moved in this way before, and I was at a loss as to how to react. This was a level of being and experiencing for which I had no vocabulary. An inner and formerly silent world was making itself seen and available through me and the other representatives, and the content was rich and expansive. I felt like a visitor in a foreign land trying to find the words and feelings to express what I was experiencing.

That was my first interaction with the knowing field. It was a personal yet inclusive experience touching upon profound universal and mystical truths. From the perspectives of neuroscience and epigenetics, the effects of that constellation were clearly logical and scientifically grounded. Yet experientially they were individually and collectively mysterious and transformative—an example of science and mysticism finding a way to happily coexist in service to the growth of the individual and the system as well as all the event's participants.

Spiritual? Yes, indeed.

This work asks for you to look within for what you need and want. It also asks you to do your work. In other words, deal with unfinished business.

As a leader, coach, parent, business associate, and human being, those around you are only able to go as far as *you* do. We lift each other up. Thus our work is never done. If you're looking for a way to elevate your spiritual practices and self-exploration, to go deep and yet wide and truly understand who you are and what your destiny is, this approach is epic.

BIG GAME CHANGERS

Can you imagine what a different place this world would be if everyone learned to access and consciously stand in the knowing field? If everyone could experience the invisible world unfolding accurately and elegantly before them and through them? If everyone could experience their unique, ancient links and the patterns and loyalties that have shaped them, accessing spaces, places, and gifts that are sacred and life changing? Can you imagine vast populations getting a sense of their greatest selves? It's all a matter of learning to look.

Be aware that when you participate in a constellation, you will probably have a direct experience of this field, and once you do, you will not and cannot ever see the world the same way. Once you have stood in the knowing field, you will be able to access it anytime you wish. Dimensionalizing isn't just a fun idea; it's a portal to embodied illumination, insight, and shift, and it is always available.

The possible uses for this work are endless: it's relevant to our private as well as professional lives, to our families and home lives as well as to our occupations and fields of study. Here are some of the places I have seen this work used effectively.

Schools are a wonderful and logical place for children to learn where and how they belong, how to reframe self-doubts and self-deprecation into self-confidence and self-respect, and how to discover their strengths and invest in their dreams. Looking ahead, systemic work and constellations could become part of regular social studies and psychology classes, and even science classes, teaching students how to experience fields of information. This work could teach students to stand in the shoes of another, building empathy; to stand on their own hopes and wishes and then feel what it's like to walk from where they are all the way into the future, to the fulfillment of their goals. Children are much more able to sense and imagine than adults.

Give them the tools to explore the world around and within themselves with curiosity, to sense the worlds of others, and to figure out how there's a place for everyone to belong, and who knows what kind of marvelous humans they'll become!

I am fortunate enough to work with many good coaches who want to be of greater service to their clients, and systemic work and constellations helps them do just that. If you are a coach of any kind—success coaching, sports coaching, executive coaching, skills coaching, life coaching—instead of just working with a small, targeted slice of a client's life, this work opens up multiple dimensions for your clients and is a real game changer for them.

Many lawyers have taken these classes and a number use the principles and approaches in their own way in their practices. With divorce cases, teaching all sides to look at what worked and what didn't empowers everyone to know what to do differently, where to grow, and how to emerge intact. Divorce can become as much of a people grower as a marriage can. Making systemic work and constellations available as a tool during divorces would invite reflection, introspection, insight, personal growth, and a healing that would positively impact many generations to come.

Finally, imagine using systemic work and constellations in local and national governmental agencies. Imagine using it at the United Nations! What if the stated intention of the UN (or any organization) were to seek to understand and grow all nations together rather than fight for small individual gains? Using constellations, delegates would no longer be able to fluff and bluff their way through global issues. A structural constellation would enable international delegates to visibly populate the path *from* the current state *to* the desired state with other countries, offering input, resources, and advice until the system relaxed and agreed. At the very least, fears, concerns, and resources could be explored dimensionally to see and feel what has the most positive effect for all parties concerned.

We are the change agents. We cannot succeed by being victims. Only by standing in the power of our own souls and teaching others how to do the same can we raise ourselves up as well as the world around us.

How we create change will change history.

Since that first constellation, I have walked in the field with clients and watched them overcome their struggles, release their smallness, set down the crutches they hobbled in on, and put away anxiety, disease, fear, poverty, addiction, and anger. I have witnessed them identify their purpose, unleash their true power, and begin to live remarkable, pain-free, abundant, joyful lives. I have seen anger give way to compassion, hatred melt into understanding, resistance transform into collaboration and innovation. When everyone and everything is seen and included, the remarkable unfolds. Deep truths and wisdom surface. For the first time, we get a sense of our true selves, and we are in awe—shocked by how good a conductor we are for the field called life to flow through us. We realize that we have been interacting with this field all our lives. We just didn't consciously realize it or know how to engage it.

Until now, we didn't realize how close and available transformation is. It is *not* in a galaxy far, far away. It is right here and now if we want it. And it's not about trying our hardest. It's about elevating our emotions, being present, and opening our heart, mind, and gut to a new possibility. It's about putting down assumptions, old patterns, and old wounds. When we come from joy, kindness, and gratitude—from relaxation and enthusiasm and excitement—we get an entirely different outcome than when we are determined to hold onto what got us stuck in the first place. All we have to do is put down our preconceived ideas and be prepared to walk into a field that is very much alive and waiting for us to awaken.

Are you wanting to transform? Are you willing? With this work, your hopes will not go unmet. Just know that the degree to which *you* are willing to transform will match your result. The more you understand and elevate your emotional blueprint, the further you will move within this mystical yet practical field and expand your life.

The ancestors protect and guard the past and offer us deep insights and wisdom. But it is up to each one of us to shape our individual destiny and thereby the destiny of our system. You may be confused, struggling, or lost. But systems speak. If you set up your system and interact with it, you will find the answers you are seeking. You will realize that the mystical is all around you and flowing through you, waiting for you to see it. And when you do, you will manifest things you never thought possible.

Beyond hidden patterns and unconscious loyalties and perceived limitations lies a field rich with possibilities simply waiting for you to touch it into reality. The blueprint is already there. The emotional DNA is yours to create. You are not limited; you only thought you were. Now that you're awake, the world will never be the same, and neither will you.

I look forward to meeting some of you at an event someday soon. I look forward to watching you unfold into the glorious being you were always meant to be. Until then, know that you are big and incredible. Your system loves you, and so does the universe.

It always did, and it always will.

ACKNOWLEDGMENTS

Despite persistent requests to share more of what I know and have experienced, writing a book had never crossed my mind. My family, including my four-legged members, have long been familiar with the glare that accompanies the suggestion that it's time to create a manual. So, writing a book was definitely not on my to-do list . . . until it was.

I have a busy and wonderful professional life working with some of the finest minds in large companies, and a busy schedule as a constellations trainer, facilitator, and practitioner. As the events increased in size and demand, so did the realization that a book was going to help so many more people to see worlds they'd never seen before and change their lives. And I dreaded the idea of writing one. I am so busy that this seemed like climbing a mountain.

The suggestion that I take some time out to write a book wasn't plausible, so instead I learned the disciplines of focusing and maximizing my time. Both were excellent, demanding teachers.

The angels conspired and in came Betsy Chasse, to and for whom I am so grateful. She is a powerful magic maker who makes wonderful things happen. She in turn introduced me to Cate Montana, who has been my sanity, my sense maker, and my guide, shaping my voice and keeping me focused and on track even when a catastrophic event threatened to derail the book. Cate, I am so grateful not just for your editing and organization but also for your creative thinking and insights, and most of all, for showing me the sacred journey of making a book. Rather than dreading it, I have learned to love it.

My deep gratitude to Lisa Hagan, who saw potential, and to Tami Simon and Sounds True for kindly inviting me into your wonderful home. I hope to be a worthy guest. Anastasia Pellouchoud, thank you for your incredible patience, and thank you Gretel Hakanson for your focus and wisdom. I am honored.

ACKNOWLEDGMENTS

Looking at where it all began, I have to thank Bert Hellinger, Jan Jacob Stam, Bibi Schreuder, and Mark Wolynn, who not only gave me insights and teaching but also a deep calling and purpose.

Thank you Claire Dagenais, Rosalba Stocco, Diana Claire Douglas, Lisa Doig, and Judy Malan for inviting me into your spaces to share what I teach.

Cecilia Rose, wherever in the universe you are right now, I know you are making a difference, and we did so much together! Tina Baker, my brainy genius and friend, thank you for your healing, kindness, and commitment to a higher way of living. Gloria Howard, you are the epitome of showing up to grow up. Brian Stovall, you show the many different ways this work can be incorporated. Sabine, your focus and humor keep me both grounded and light. Betsey, your techy genius also started the expansion. To HJ Nelson, who gave me a chance, and Cheryl DeSantis, a heart-centered leader of note: thank you.

A special thank you to Barry Goldstein and Woody, who took me to a whole new level of professionalism and kept me focused and striving. I can't wait to show the world what you have worked with me to create and to continue to make more of that magic together.

Thank you to my mother, brother, and daughter for your belief in me. It's so appreciated and provides the juice at the end of long days.

Transformational thinking is alive and well in large companies, and it shows. I am thankful to each and every one of you who invites me in and dares to shape your organizations—and so the world—in higher ways.

I have to acknowledge all the transformation teachers out there paving the way and showing what is possible when we dare to think beyond what we see in front of us, dare to align the power of the heart, head, and gut. You are the shapers of the world we want to see, and I honor you. Without you all, I would not have dared to write such a book.

To the countless clients and attendees at my events: without all of you, none of this would have been possible. Your courage, wisdom, and insights created this book. You now know that transformation is in your own hands, and you know how to use it well.

Finally, to the knowing field and all that it contains, and the quantum field and all that is possible, without you both the journeys inward and outward would not have been possible, and neither would this book.

Thank you.

NOTES

Chapter 1. The System:
A Treasure Chest of Possibilities

1 Bert Hellinger, *No Waves Without the Ocean* (Heidelberg, Germany: Carl Auer International, 2006).

Chapter 3. The Science Behind
Systemic Work and Constellations

1 Arthur C. Clarke, *Profiles of the Future: An Inquiry Into the Limits of the Possible* (New York: Harper & Row, 1973).

2 Milton Erickson, *In the Room with Milton H. Erickson, MD, Vol. 1, (Oct. 3–5, 1979)*, produced by Jane Parsons-Fein (New York: Parsons-Fein Press, 2014), 12 CD set.

3 Frank W. Stahnisch and Robert Nitsch, "Santiago Ramón y Cajal's Concept of Neuronal Plasticity: The Ambiguity Lives On," *Trends in Neurosciences* 25, no. 11 (2002): 589–591.

4 Donald Hebb, *The Organization of Behavior: A Neuropsychological Theory* (New York: John Wiley and Sons, 1949).

5 Norman Doidge, MD, *The Brain That Changes Itself: Stories of Personal Triumph from the Frontiers of Brain Science* (New York: Penguin Books, 2007).

6 Maxwell Maltz, *Psycho-Cybernetics* (New York: Simon and Schuster, 1960); P. Lally, C. H. M. van Jaarsveld, H. W. W. Potts, and J. Wardle, "How Are Habits Formed: Modeling Habit Formation in the Real World," *European Journal of Social Psychology* 40, no. 6 (2010): 998–1009.

7   Yildez Sethi, *Rapid Core Healing: Pathways to Growth and Emotional Healing* (Seattle: CreateSpace, 2016).

8   Kathryn Gudsnuk and Frances A. Champagne, "Epigenetic Influence of Stress and the Social Environment," *ILAR Journal* 53, no. 3–4 (December 2012): 279–288.

9   Sarah Gangi, Alessandro Talamo, and Stefano Ferrcuti, "The Long-Term Effects of Extreme War-Related Trauma on the Second Generation of Holocaust Survivors," *Violence and Victims* 24, no. 5 (2009): 687–700.

10 Laura C. Schulz, "The Dutch Hunger Winter and the Developmental Origins of Health and Disease," *Proceedings of the National Academy of Sciences of the United States of America (PNAS)* 107, no. 39 (September 28, 2010): 16757–16758.

11 Connie X. Wang, Isaac A. Hilburn, Daw-An Wu, et. al, "Transduction of the Geomagnetic Field as Evidenced from alpha-Band Activity in the Human Brain," *eNeuro* 6, no. 2 (March 18, 2019), doi.org/10.1523/ENEURO.0483-18.2019.

12 Rupert Sheldrake, *A New Science of Life: The Hypothesis of Morphic Resonance* (Rochester, VT: Park Street Press, 1995).

13 The Copenhagen interpretation was the first general attempt by Danish physicist Niels Bohr and German theoretical physicist Werner Heisenberg to understand the world of atoms as represented by quantum mechanics. Between 1926 and 1927, Heisenberg served as Bohr's assistant in Copenhagen, where they formulated this fundamental uncertainty principle. Their principle came to be colloquially known in scientific circles as the Copenhagen interpretation.

14 B. R. Grad, "A Telekinetic Effect on Plant Growth II. Experiments Involving Treatment of Saline in Stopped Bottles," *International Journal of Parapsychology* 6 (1964): 473–498.

15 Lynne McTaggert, *The Intention Experiment: Using Your Thoughts to Change Your Life and the World* (New York: Atria, 2007).

16 University of South Hampton, "Study Reveals Substantial Evidence of Holographic Universe," January 31, 2017, southampton.ac.uk/news/2017/01/holographic-universe.page.

ABOUT THE AUTHOR

Judy Wilkins-Smith is an international organizational, individual, and family patterns expert; a systemic coach, trainer, and facilitator; and a motivational speaker and founder of System Dynamics for Individuals & Organizations. For eighteen years she has been assisting high-profile, high-performance individuals, Fortune 500 executives and leadership teams, legacy families, and heads of state. As a trainer and facilitator, she is advancing systemic work and constellations beyond the role of healing into the realms of transformation, holding public and master classes throughout the US, Canada, South Africa, the UK, Australia, and Mexico. Born and raised in South Africa, she now resides in Texas.

ABOUT SOUNDS TRUE

Sounds True is a multimedia publisher whose mission is to inspire and support personal transformation and spiritual awakening. Founded in 1985 and located in Boulder, Colorado, we work with many of the leading spiritual teachers, thinkers, healers, and visionary artists of our time. We strive with every title to preserve the essential "living wisdom" of the author or artist. It is our goal to create products that not only provide information to a reader or listener but also embody the quality of a wisdom transmission.

For those seeking genuine transformation, Sounds True is your trusted partner. At SoundsTrue.com you will find a wealth of free resources to support your journey, including exclusive weekly audio interviews, free downloads, interactive learning tools, and other special savings on all our titles.

To learn more, please visit SoundsTrue.com/freegifts or call us toll-free at 800.333.9185.

sounds true
WAKING UP THE WORLD